Witness Book 20
Christian Experience Series

Death and other Living things

Nathan R. Kollar

Pflaum/Standard
Dayton, Ohio 45439

Nihil Obstat:
Reverend Joseph B. Collins, S.S.
Censor Deputatus

Imprimatur:
Patrick Cardinal O'Boyle
Apostolic Administrator
Archdiocese of Washington
April 3, 1973

Library of Congress Catalog Card Number 73-87808
© 1973 National Center of Religious Education,
Washington, D.C.
ISBN 0-8278-2127-1
Book Designed by Tim Potter

CONTENTS

Preface   4

1 Death   6
2 Dying   22
3 Sickness, Dying, and the Church   36
4 The Living and the Death   48
5 The Living, the Dead, and the Church   58
6 Preparing the Children   68
7 Preparing Yourself   80
8 Other Things: Faith and Hope   88
   Appendix A: Scriptural References   98
   Appendix B: Preparations for Death   102
   Appendix C: Celebration   110
   Notes   116

PREFACE

If one is to breathe the freedom of life, he must face the reality of death. Death is a part of life, for mature living requires many deaths. These pages are concerned with death; but as you will soon see, this is a direct concern with life.

What you find here is the result of much discussion, reading, and experience. It began with a doctoral thesis dealing with the concept of sickness and anointing in the Church of England and ended with a friend's request to write a study guide for adult education. In between those two points were the three years required to write the thesis (1965-67), two semesters of teaching a graduate seminar on "Death, Suffering, and the Church" (1969-71), and three years 1969-71, of seeing impersonal death destroy individuals in urban slums.

This is not a book to be read with the eyes and argued with the mind. It is based upon the idea that a person can understand an author only if he has an experience similar to the author's. You are therefore asked to "do" certain actions in the hope that you will share some of my experiences. The book is also based upon the concept that all education is self-education. Education is not a process of passing on information; rather, it is the process of providing the opportunities for self-formation. I believe that this occurs both in private reflection and in community discussion. Consequently, each chapter ends with suggestions for personal reflection and suggestions for group reflection. If you are to understand what I mean, *truly* understand, then you must carry out these reflections.

The suggestions for personal reflection can best be carried out as follows: Buy a notebook or a diary. Read each question and jot down ideas as they come to you before you begin to filter them through your fears, images, expectations, etc. No need for complete sentences; just jot down your ideas when they come and as they come. After writing them out, go back over them and reflect on what you have written. Perhaps, if you get the chance, you might share these intimate reflections with someone you trust.

The group reflections should be held regularly, about once a week. They are designed to give everyone an opportunity to express his mind and feelings in regard to the matter at hand. No one should be forced to say what he feels. Freedom should be the criterion of each discussion group: freedom to speak, to listen, to act.

My hope is that through these pages, you may see death as yet another living thing. My thanks to all who contributed by written or spoken words to what follows, especially to my wife who contributed her life and light to the struggle which gave these thoughts birth.

CHAPTER I—DEATH

Death belongs to life as birth does.
The walk is in the raising of the foot as in
the laying of it down.

Tagore, *Stray Birds* CCLXVII

We seldom see death. How many dead people have you seen this year? Last year? There are old folks' homes where the chronologically dead sleep away their last years. There are hospitals where the violence of sudden death is washed down sterile drains. Death in Asia or the Near East happens "over there." Cowboys are murdered on a distant T.V. prairie. They die quickly, with few complications, to allow the sponsor time enough to sell his product. One of the most profound and far-reaching occurrences in the life of any human being is whispered about . . . neglected.

In the 1968 Paul Almond movie, *Isabel*, one of the principal actors calmly explains to his niece that his body will be placed in the grave next to that of her mother. He takes another step, points to the next plot of land, and says, "This is for you." Nervous twitters of laughter, restless movements, and talking drown the subsequent dialogue. A torrid love scene or a violent murder does not produce so much uneasiness. The only conclusion from such empty reactions is that not only sex education but also *death* education is necessary today.

Death education is necessary because we ignore death. Birds die. Leaves fall from the tree and die. Earth is fresh, productive, and life-bearing because things and animals die. But our culture ignores death. It is as if our entire world lives without any relationship to death.

We and our children exist in a world physically and psychologically different from that of our forefathers. Ours is a world directed more by medical men than medicine men; more by men in white coats than men in white collars. These men immortalize us in sperm and egg banks, program our genetic material, or freeze us for tomorrow. They give us novocaine to drill a tooth and morphine to probe deeper.

Who prepares us for death today? Surely the friendly insurance man, funeral home, and apocalyptic billboards are not equipping us. Most of the messages we get premise (not promise) everlasting life on earth—in soft, clean, hairless, deodorized, fragrant original skin.

Life expectancy at birth in mid-eighteenth century was twenty-five years. In France, for example, 430 to 440 out of 1,000 lived to marriage age. Half of the marriages reached their fifteenth anniversary. At fourteen years of age, the average child experienced the death of a parent. He was one of five children, only half of whom lived to see their fifteenth birthday. Later, as the father of five children, he saw two or three die before his own death, at age fifty-two. He had survived two or three famines, long periods of serious food shortage, and several epidemics that cut down large numbers of persons in his community. In former times, death was in the midst of life as the cemetery was in the middle of the village. Since then, death, poverty, and suffering are retreating.

Most of us do not encounter death frequently. We take for granted that contagious illnesses can be cured or prevented; our parents did not. We take for granted that infants will grow up, thrive, and outlive us; our grandparents used to bury many children. We take for granted that an anesthetic will spare us the pain of toothache, surgery, and childbirth; but our great-grandparents accepted pain as a part of life . . . and of death.

Our forefathers could assume that the world would still be here for many generations to follow; we cannot be so sure. Our ancestors' way of thinking enabled them to cope with a cruel Providence that robbed them of their loved ones roughly and too soon. We have technically pulled the wires from premature death and refocused our philosophical concerns on man's present life and not his afterlife.

North Americans have become separated from the orthodox views of life and death that guided prior generations. The bereaved are now doubly so, for those of the new technological society are more and more without the comforting belief in an afterlife.

Many people have to face death without aids of any kind. Society no longer provides them with the Christian mores that so long sustained them. As a consequence, they try to avoid facing the emotional pain of death; in doing so, they court serious emotional disorder.

Why are so many trying to ignore death?

One reason is that without a concept of afterlife it is harder to face death directly because those who traditionally prepared people for death, or helped them handle it when it happened, are not present.

Second, nonemotionalism is more and more becoming a cherished and respected fact of life in our culture. Facing death realistically demands that we face the emotions of death: those surrounding the fact that "I" will die or the reality that everyone I love will die. Death is a very emotional situation and, among those afraid of their emotions, it is better ignored.

Third, the media—in particular, television—have made war and killing seem almost frivolous and not the human tragedies that they are. Because they happen so easily, so far away, and with such dispatch it is easy to ignore them. The media have also presented us with the youth cult. Death happens to the old. What we should be interested in is the vitality of the "now" generation, so the advertising agents tell us through the media. Any hint of death would destroy this focus on youth. Because of our great concern with youth and because the young seldom die in our culture, death is rarely heeded in ordinary life.

These are three reasons why many ignore death. There may be more, but the fact is that people are not facing it. For instance, one million people in the United States have had a close family member either killed or seriously wounded in Vietnam. Yet one finds no conscious mourning in America. Will such neglect of death leave us without an understanding of death?

Each of us will die. None of us knows what our own personal death is. Perhaps we have seen someone close to us die and have a lasting memory of that death. Death, though a reality, is a mysterious reality. It is beyond our total comprehension. Before its reality and possibility, we stand with naked instinct and trembling reason.

The exact moment of death is difficult to determine. How does one determine death? Is it the loss of consciousness? Does it occur when the heart stops? When the brain no longer functions? The medical profession is having a difficult time with this question, especially since the art of transplants has developed so extensively. A committee at Harvard University, under the direction of Dr. Henry K. Beecher, lists four criteria for an irreversible coma that terminates in death.[1] The criteria proposed are 1) unreceptivity and nonresponsiveness, described as "deep unconsciousness" with no response to external stimuli or internal needs; 2) no movements or breathing; 3) no reflexes; 4) a flat electroencephalogram (EEG) showing no electric activity in the brain. This committee, and the vast majority of medical people who have accepted their findings, would see death as determined by one's consciousness. I do not want to become engaged in attempting a comprehensive definition of death. Instead let us speak only about what I would call biological death.

Biologically, natural death is not a sudden event but a slow process. From a biological point of view, we begin to age and die as soon as we are born. But the complete death of the individual takes place only after the last of the millions of cells that compose his body are dead. A cell dies when its protoplasmic activity ceases. Thus death, from this point of view, is the destruction of the cellular organization. Although the cells die, and thereby bring about the death of the individual, the atoms that make up the cells are not destroyed. They pass into other cells, other individuals, and it is in this sense that we can effectively speak of an essential kinship among all living creatures. The atoms that are today part of my corporeal makeup may one day be shared by animals and plants, or perhaps other men.

The cell itself is a complex organism and as such cannot be considered immortal. Only protoplasm is. Neither science nor magic can prevent the death of cells and the organism composed of them; at most, their death can be delayed. It is not unlikely that the length of human life will one day be doubled or even tripled. But *natural* death has no final remedy.

Only death in old age can be called "natural" according to our definition. And this applies only if it does not result from illness, as is frequently the case. Illness often proves mortal because the patient is already on the threshold of natural death and would probably have died soon anyway. The death of the young, whose cells are in a constant process of renewal, is always accidental. Hygiene and other measures can diminish the risk of accidental death and, thanks to these, the mortality rate among the young has appreciably declined in the past century. But it is always difficult to specify the exact cause of death. Most medical certificates leave room for four options: natural, homicide, suicide, or accidental.

Species as well as individuals die. The only thing that escapes death in the empirical order is life itself. And even that is endangered today by nuclear explosives.

Each of us has the right to want to live forever and seek ways and means of avoiding the fatality of death. This is only natural. But as soon as we view matters from the point of view of life in general, we must recognize that death is necessary to make the emergence of new individuals and species possible. If everyone and everything that was born lived, the world would be piled high with life.

To obviate the absolute necessity of death, the reproduction of living things would have had to stop soon after it began. The consequence of this would be the absence of all growth, all evolution of the species. Man, the result of a long evolutionary process, would never have appeared on earth or, on the assumption that he was "created" on the sixth day, would never have evolved to his present state. In a word, we can conceive of the absence of death only in an entirely static universe where a determined number of members of different species would have been created in the beginning and remained constant for the duration. I do not know whether such a universe would have been preferable to our own. But there is no doubt that in an evolutionary universe death is a necessity.

Death *is* a necessity. Yours, mine, your family's. Not only is it a necessity, but some day it will be a fact. Does it sound morbid to think about your own death and the death of others? It seems that "death" is never *our* death. It is always someone else's. It is true that none of us will know death until we experience it ourselves. The closest we can get to knowing our own death is experiencing the death of someone we love. In sharing this death we come the closest to knowing what our own death will be like.

Ann was a young girl of five, full of life and curiosity. Her grandparents had died when she was four, but she never adverted to that fact even though she had loved them a great deal while they were alive. Ann had a small kitten which had been given to her on her fifth birthday. The kitten followed her everywhere. One day Ann climbed a tree and somehow got the kitten up in the tree with her. While playing with her pet, she accidentally knocked it out of the tree. The kitten fell, hitting its head on a brick wall beneath the tree, and was killed instantly. Ann was terribly shaken by the event. Her mother told her that the kitten was dead. Only then did she understand the meaning of her grandparents' death. The dead no longer move; they cannot talk; they are cold. They are disposed of as her pet is disposed of. In the following days she asked many questions such as "Will mother and father die?" "Do all people die?" And, finally, "Will Ann die?" Death of those close to us can help us understand our own death.

Yet we never really know what death is until we die. Even sharing deeply the death of someone we love dearly is not enough. Death, like life, is essentially very mysterious. No one knows exactly what it is like.

Generally, the concept "death" may mean 1) a complete cessation of all experience, 2) a termination of bodily processes without cessation of experience, 3) an interruption until the "resurrection," or 4) a continuation of life under more favorable circumstances. These views take away none of the mystery. Practically, we can divide views on death into two extremes: First, death ends all, and second, death is not the end. Between these two points of view, one finds many theories of the nature of death. I would like to present one view on death. It is not the only Christian view. There are others. But the following reflections are offered in the spirit of one Christian to another by a person who has spent some time reflecting and thinking about the theories of death.

At the outset, it is important to realize that talking about and meditating on death are valuable and meaningful when they help us transfigure death. We can moan and groan about our own death, but all the moaning and groaning will make little difference unless we face the fact that we will die. Death does have a meaning for us whether we are aware of it or not. Our choice is to accept the meaning of death implanted in our subconscious at childhood or to bring this meaning to the surface and consciously or subconsciously accept or reject it. We must choose, or someone (or thing) will choose for us.

Man is built for life, not for death. At the same time, ideas presented by Freud, with his death-wish, or Heidegger, with his being-for-death, do have something to tell us. What they state emphatically is that man is oriented to death from the moment he is born.

This makes sense when we think about it. After

birth, there really is no event quite as catastrophic as our death. Our vision of that death will be the vision of our life. If we see death as the cessation of life, then how will we see our daily existence? Will it have any significance? If we see death as a new birth, a change in life, what will that do to our vision of daily living? We live as we die. Or to reverse the sentence, and thus make it more familiar, *we die as we live.*

An example of how a person's death can concretize his life can be found in a story related by Canon Pym, a chaplain:

When I entered the cell I began to suspect that my worst fears were going to be realized. The convict seemed to have no redeeming feature, no vestige of manhood, as he sat on his bunk whining that he was innocent of the crime for which he was about to suffer. To this I could only respond by saying that if he was innocent he would not be the first innocent person to be condemned to death. Then came the surprising rejoinder. On the wall hung a crucifix and the prisoner, pointing to it, blurted out: 'Yes, but he was perfectly good; there was a point in him dying; but what's the point of the death of a man like me?' "[2]

If this is how the prisoner saw his death, how did he see his life?

When we speak of death, we are talking about it in a larger context than biology. It is more than a biological event which we passively accept. We can choose it, as we choose other things in life. Our life is made up of choices. Ultimately our personality is constituted by our choices. From the fundamental choice of life itself to the more mundane selection of what to eat, the act of choosing is the line that slowly sketches our personality. Throughout our lifetime we have chosen a job, a mate, friends. These choices enter into our life. They become part of us.

Death creeps into our life in many ways. Sickness is one prime example. In a serious sickness we come face to face with the possibility of death. How do we react? How many times, too, are we faced with the choice of serving ourself or others? Isn't it a preview of death when we are faced with the choice of accepting another as important and sacrificing our present concerns? Isn't this close to a destruction of self? A dying? Who is more vital and involved with life: the individual who is giving his time and interest, or the one who lies safely behind his walls, afraid of everything outside? Who *does* face death: the person who faces the possibility of all of his plans collapsing as he acts, or the one who keeps life's plans and possibilities locked up in a safe place?

There is death in every "now." And there is life in every "now." In our daily choices, we implicitly or explicitly prepare ourselves for the death-choice. In our attitudes of choosing today, we prepare ourselves for our choosing tomorrow. Man is made by his choices. He evidences one of the constitutive aspects of his being in choosing freely. Death, too, must be one of these conscious choices. Notice I am not saying that we should kill ourselves, but simply that all of us have a choice to choose death, however it occurs in our life, or to cry out against it as it comes to take us. What shall it be: a human decision of choice, of accepting a meaningful death, or of forgetting about it until it happens?

"One who chooses to live as a Christian chooses to die as a Christian." When we hear words like these, we often imagine the last ministrations of a priest or a minister, who whispers words of eternal comfort. In the context we are concerned with here, however, a Christian death refers to an attitude of mind more than to such imaginings: an attitude of mind which sees our daily life involved with dying and rising (living) with Christ.

Every Christian has become one with Jesus Christ. We are the visible expression of Christ within time and space. In baptism we have become identified with Christ in such a way that Paul can say we are the body of Christ. Christ walked this earth many centuries ago. He walks it today. But the difference in the way He "walks" is found in the different representations of His body. One body is that which has arms, legs, hair and eyes, which manifests Him to others. The other body is the Christian community, the Church, which also manifests Christ.

True life exists when we live joined in the vitality of this body and when we act with Christ as our model. All else is death. Our life, if Christian, is lived in the process of continually being baptized into the life and imitation of Christ. It began with baptism.

For surely you know this: when we were baptized into union with Christ Jesus, we were baptized into union with his death. By our baptism, then, we were buried with him and shared his death in order that, just as Christ was raised from death by the glorious power of the Father, so also we might live a new life. For if we become one with him in dying as he did, in the same way we shall be one with him by being raised to life as he was. For we know this our old being has been put to death with Christ on his cross in order that the power of the sinful self might be destroyed, so that we should no longer be the slaves of sin. For when a person

dies he is set free from the power of sin. If we
have died with Christ, we believe that we will
also live with him. For we know that Christ has
been raised from the dead and will never die
again—death has no more power over him. The
death he died was death to sin, once and for all
and the life he now lives is life to God. In the
same way you are to think of yourselves as dead
to sin but alive to God in union with Christ
Jesus. (Rom 6:3-11)
And what was begun in baptism is continued throughout life as we partake of the reality of being Christ's body.

. . . we hold this treasure in earthen vessels,
to show that the transcendent power belongs to
God and not to us. We are afflicted in every way
but not crushed; perplexed but not driven to
despair; persecuted but not forsaken; struck
down but not destroyed; always carrying in the
body the death of Jesus, so that the life of Jesus
may also be manifested in our bodies. For while
we live we are always being given up to death
for Jesus's sake, so that the life of Jesus may be
manifested in our mortal flesh. (2 Cor 4:7-11)

Death, then, is something we choose. In baptism we have already chosen to die with Christ, to live with Christ. In baptismal faith we recognize that Jesus lives, that He is the firstborn of the new creation and that all of us as new creatures are also being born into a new life. The process of continual birth is something that is constantly happening in our life. It happens until we are completely born so that our death day can be called, as the early Christians designated it, our birthday. Christ lives, though He died. We will live even though we die. How? What manner of living? What will we know and love once we have died? These and thousands of other questions have collected centuries of answers. It is enough for us to affirm what we know: Death is not the end!

But what does it mean "to die in Christ"? As is evident, the word "death" in the context above means two things: 1) a cessation of physical activity and life and 2) the conscious acceptance of this fact with all of the consequences. In turn, I see daily events as symbolic of final death. These daily symbolic events truly manifest and effect that final death. They manifest and effect it in such a way that by looking at our daily deaths we can come to an understanding of our final death, and by looking at our final death we can understand our daily ones. If these things are understood, then we can begin to look into the meaning of "to die in Christ."

Let us begin with the daily death. When we are aware of what is happening around us (aware of the joy and the sorrow, anguish and celebration, physical pain and physical well-being) such awareness presents us with an opportunity to open ourselves to what is happening, to participate in our world. Conversely, it presents us with an opportunity to close ourselves off, to retreat into our own embryonic ball of selfhood. The act of going out is risk-filled. We have to "die" to some of our desires and securities in order to breathe deeply the freshness of the experience in which we become immersed. Whenever we open ourselves to another person, such "death" occurs. It must happen in order to bring life. To understand another, we need a certain basic empathy, a true listening, a sensitivity to his entire world. Without this, we cannot participate in his life. For example, to listen to a child the way we listen to an adult is to cut ourselves off from the true living the child offers us (and vice versa). A certain faith is necessary when we allow ourselves really to become involved with another human being. But as a result of this faith, sometimes given in fear and trembling, we can awaken to a new life.

This basic attitude, which is grounded in our daily experiences, is brought to our relation with Jesus Christ. He is not some *thing* to be manipulated or bowed to. Rather he is real. He is a person. He is alive. Alive for us. "To die in Christ" daily is to be alive to all that is good and beautiful. It is to be alive! By being sensitive to His working in the world around us, we must die; to listen to His word from the lips of others we must die. We must become aware.

If this attitude is present in life, then the final death will be a fulfillment of our whole life (which is a constant mixture of life and death). Dying in Christ will mean that we die as we have lived: in the name of Christ Jesus. Will it make things easier? Perhaps. Faith will still be necessary. Death loses none of its horror, its emptiness, its isolation. But we believe in this person, Jesus. We know that with this final death we will break through to a new life. From the womb of this world, we will break into a new one.

Suggestions for Personal Reflection:

1. Take a walk and observe the death and life around you. After the walk, sit down and enter into your diary what you have seen.
2. Whose death do you fear the most? What do you enjoy most in others?
3. Have you allowed anyone to live this week?
4. Choose a specific action which will bring life to the one closest to you. Resolve to perform this action regularly this week.

Suggestions for Group Reflection:

1. Do you think we choose death?
2. What are some ways to become aware of people? Things? God?
3. Do you think death education is necessary?
4. What are the best things in life?

CHAPTER II—DYING

"What man shall live and not see death?"

(Ps 89:49)

A person sick in bed is a scene familiar enough to all of us. Some of us may have been in the presence of a dying parent or child. Innately, it seems, we know the games to play with dying people. The dying person responds to our games. Everyone avoids reference to "that" lest it disturb the patient. But how do we know that the patient does not want to talk about "that"? Are we afraid to become involved in the feelings of the dying person? Are we avoiding talking about death because of the dying person or because of our fear of death?

So we put on a mask, enter the room, give a phony smile, and say a few cute words like, "In a few weeks you will be out jogging in the morning." The patient responds with a phony titter and feels depressed when we leave. He senses that another loved one is refusing to take his dying seriously. Another person is deserting him as he goes down into the valley of death.

Dying is difficult for everyone: the patient, the family, the medical staff. Each has his reasons. They may range from personal to financial, from deep-felt loss to a gnawing sense of failure at not being able to keep the individual alive. In what follows I briefly treat the dying-situation as it affects these individuals.

Elisabeth Kübler-Ross in her book *On Death and Dying* (New York: Macmillan, 1970) discusses quite extensively the experiences of the dying. Much of what follows is based upon her findings, my personal experience, and the experience of those who participated in my seminars on "Death, Suffering, and the Church."

Dying usually takes place in hospitals. More and more these have become large impersonal bins into which are poured bodies to be cared for and saved. Dying begins here for it is here that many people are overcome with the awesomeness of what lies before them. Dr. Kübler-Ross has discovered, by talking with persons who were terminally ill, that a person goes through five phases of emotional reaction to death.

The dying patient's first reaction is *denial*: "No, not me!" The response serves an important function: It allows the patient to collect himself and, with time, to mobilize other, less radical defenses. This reaction usually occurs when the doctor shares his knowledge of the impending death with the patient. Often the patient does not hear the words, not because they are not stated clearly but because he is not ready to deal with them. Or he'll hear the words but merely repeat them like a small child learning to spell by rote memory.

Denial eventually yields to a deep *anger* crying, "Why me?" As a 50-year-old dentist reminisced, "An old man whom I have known ever since I was a little kid came down the street. He is 82 years old, and he is of no earthly use as far as we mortals can tell. And the thought hit me strongly, 'Now why couldn't it have been old George instead of me?'" Many times the religious person becomes "irreligious." "Why does God do this to me?" "Why am I being punished?" "I have tried to live a good life. Why?" The patient strikes out at any available target: the nurse who "failed" to carry out some procedure, the doctor who did not diagnose the illness "properly" a year ago. Anger at God is displaced as the person comes realistically to acknowledge the fact that death is near and he cannot fight it.

Resentment is succeeded in turn by bargaining,

which is a campaign, often undetectable, to somehow stay execution of sentence. The difficult patient may abruptly turn cooperative. The reward he seeks for good behavior is an extension of life. Mrs. Kübler-Ross cites the poignant case of an opera singer, her face ravaged by a fatal malignancy, who begged for a chance to sing one last time; thus death would have to wait. She did "sing" by telling about her feelings and thoughts of death and dying. And death did wait until she had finished.

In this negotiating process the patient does have a part in determining when he will die. When he realizes that the illness is fatal, he still may have some unfinished business. He may wish to wait until a graduation, a wedding, or someone's visit. Death can be made to wait. But not forever. Like a child who promises never to hit his sister again if he is not punished, so after staying the hand of death the patient tries again.

It is at this stage, too, that many bargains with God are made. There is promise of "a life dedicated to God," or "a life in the service of the Church," in exchange for some additional time. Often these promises are associated with quiet guilt and should never be brushed away. Rather they should be taken advantage of to assist the patient to see the motives underlying his bargaining.

After the bargaining stage, the patient generally sinks into a profound *depression.* This stage has a positive side. The patient is weighing the fearful price of death, preparing himself to accept the loss of everything and everyone he loves. It is anticipating the loss of all. It is a depression similar to the one a widow might go through when she experiences the loneliness of separation from her husband.

When the sick person is sad over such total loss, it

is inane to tell him to look at the sunny side of the situation. Rather he should be allowed to express himself and his sorrow. It is a real sorrow. In a short time he will be dead. Our presence and concern are what are important. Prior to this time, the depression may have been of a different variety. It may have been a concern for those he was leaving behind. In *that* stage of depression he should be assured that all is taken care of and that things are not as bad as they seem. In *this* instance, however, holding the hand of the patient, stroking his hair, or praying with him are all supports in this extreme of depression. One does not talk a lot. One's presence is enough.

The final stage is *acceptance,* when at last the condemned patient bows to his sentence and is prepared to die with dignity. One woman who had fought death for some time stated it quite simply: "I am ready now and not afraid any more." She died the next day.

Such acceptance should not be understood as some kind of euphoria. Quite the contrary, *passivity* describes the state much better. It is a time when the individual's circle of interest diminishes. He wishes to be left to himself and his world and not to be interrupted by the problems of others. Many times the patient's family misinterprets this as rejection. This is not so. It is especially at this point that the family, rather than the patient, need help to understand what is happening. The family must come to realize that when a patient finally works through to the point where he is able to face his death, he will gradually detach himself from this world.

But before we speak about the family, the attitude which forms the core of the terminally ill patient's existence must be underlined. This core is the attitude of hope. In an age in which religious faith is crumbling, hope provides the means of enduring the months and years of suffering and living with the foreknowledge of death. Hope persists through all the stages of dying. It is the feeling that all this must have some meaning and will eventually pay off if the sickness can be endured for a little longer. Many people around the patient will give up hope at the wrong time. When the hospital staff and family convey an atmosphere of hopelessness during the initial stages of the illness, or they project the thought that the person is useless, then he may as well be dead. What they must do is maintain hope with the patient, but not to reinforce the hope when he finally accepts his death. At this stage there may be an opposite problem: The family may not accept the patient's dying. Now it is the family that needs help from someone who is aware of what is happening.

Dying ends in death. And there are those who still live, who are affected by this death, who have lived through each stage of the dying process. They stand with their own thoughts, guilts, blessings. In ever-widening circles people stand affected by the dying person's suffering and impending death.

First, there are the near relatives: husband (father), wife (mother), children (brothers and sisters). Suddenly there is something new in their lives. Like a new baby which has all the attention focused on it, the terminally ill patient becomes someone different because of his impending death. The life of the family rotates around him. He, perhaps unknowingly, controls the time, travel, and involvements of the family. He has to be visited and cared for. The hospital bills have to be paid. The hospital and the patient's room become an extension of the home.

Anyone caught in this vortex of death finds himself

in a bewildering swirl of unfamiliar activity. All at once, new roles are forced upon him. If the husband is sick, the wife may be faced with added difficulties of finances, business matters, threats to security, and the burden of being a lone parent. The husband, on the other hand, may find himself taking care of the children, serving his wife, and tending to the thousand other things that make a house a home. New thoughts have to be thought, new plans made, and ultimately a new life must evolve from the situation.

The goal of all concerned should be to help everyone (patient included) face the crisis together in order to achieve acceptance of death. How difficult it is for patients to face impending and anticipated death when the family is not ready to "let go." Many times the family will implicitly or explicitly prevent the patient from accepting his death. A number of practical considerations may help us understand what is happening and reach this goal.

First, we cannot function efficiently in the constant awareness of the illness. The various members of the family should take a break, relax, get away from the atmosphere of illness. Many think it out of order to go to a movie, go bowling, or enjoy any form of recreation when someone is dying. Quite the contrary, one must be able to "get away" for a while. In addition, the illness allows for a gradual adjustment and change toward the kind of home it is going to be when the patient is no longer around. The energies of the family will be taxed many times during the illness. Members should ration these energies as economically as possible.

Second, communication should continue throughout the illness. The terminally ill person is alive. He is a human being. He should be treated as such from the first moment that his sickness is known. The overcoming of the problem of sharing the news of his illness sets the stage for all subsequent encounters. But our sharing this news with him will depend upon 1) our own attitude and ability to face terminal illness and death and 2) the patient and his personality. Almost invariably the patient will react to the news as he has reacted to other events in his past life. One should wait for the right moment to tell him. As with so many things in life, there are opportune moments to speak of death. The patient's disposition should be taken into consideration when the news is about to be shared with him.

Communication of the patient's feelings to the family and the family to the patient are essential if all are properly to prepare for death. Many of the difficulties which surface during these times may be due to feelings of guilt. Who hasn't angrily said, "Drop dead!" to someone close? Or perhaps there were other wishes or actions that the family members feel may have caused the sickness or the present situation. If possible, these feelings should be brought to the surface and resolved.

Third, family members should recognize that they, too, undergo their own stages of adjustment to the illness:

1) They may deny the fact that there is such an illness in the family. They may begin to wander about in search of a better diagnosis, whether it be from a doctor, a fortune teller, or a faith healer. But sooner or later, they must face reality. The facing of reality is not so traumatic among those who have talked and cried together.

2) Anger, resentment, guilt—these three emotions may all be wrapped into one as the family strikes out

at the doctor or nursing staff: anger at those who diagnosed the illness, resentment at those who prevent them from being with the patient, guilt over past wrongs and personal omissions. Again, if possible, the family should be helped to see the true cause of their anger, resentment, and guilt.

3) Preparatory grief over the proximate death—this stage of grief is similar to the patient's. At the same time, it is an opportunity to express one's grief. Keeping a "stiff upper lip" at this moment usually causes an even deeper experience of grief after death.

4) Finally, to repeat once again, communication is most important. If the members of the family can share these emotions they will gradually face the reality of the impending separation and come to an acceptance of it together. Even such things as extraordinary expenses for life-support systems many times are resolved when the patient feels free to express the wish to die rather than to be plunged into the myriad machines, pipes, tubes that may be necessary for continuing life.

The entire question of whether a medical staff should prolong or shorten the dying process is difficult. The medical staff is trained for life, not death. Yet many times in the case of terminally ill patients, they must face the problem of allowing or hastening death. Their job and decisions are not easy ones in this age of science.

Today we can prolong life in unheard-of ways. In order to live, the patient must turn over his life to the various machines, tubes, electrical currents, and other life-support systems. When all is said and done, one wonders how *human* a life is that pulsates only with the aid of these systems. Further, one wonders, what is the obligation to prolong such a life?

There are many theories about the right of oneself, society, or an individual over life. It would seem that the school of ethics which holds that one is bound to use ordinary means for sustaining life is the most sensible. It provides a helpful distinction for making life-death decisions.

. . . a procedure is ordinary if it is reasonable considering the condition of the patient. It would be considered extraordinary if it is exceptionally costly, unusual, painful or dangerous considering the condition of the patient. An example would be use of a kidney machine. In technological terms it is an extraordinary procedure. Yet if the kidney machine returned the person to many years of reasonably normal and productive life, you might want to call it an ordinary procedure. On the other hand, if the kidney machine patient found himself to be a slave to the machine, found that the machine made life inhuman, found that life was meaningless and its maintenance extremely painful and costly, then the procedure might be seen as extraordinary. (R. Veatch, "Death and Dying," *U.S. Catholic* (April 1972), p. 11).

If what is said above is true, then whose judgment is to prevail regarding the facts of the case and the means of prolonging life? The doctor's? The patient's? Can the doctor neglect the patient's wishes? These moral questions are complicated by the declared disagreement among doctors as to whether patients have the right to be allowed to die or whether patients should be helped to die. A survey of doctors on this question found that 40 percent were in favor of giving patients the right to decide that they be allowed to die; 30 percent said they would permit the death if asked

(*Ibid.*, p. 12).

It would seem that the best solution is that the situation be left in the patient's hands, with the provision that the doctor or medical staff can always refuse to participate in the act.

As one can see, there is no easy solution to this problem. On one side it might seem that we are approving suicide by making the statement above. On the other side it might seem that we are accepting a univocal concept of "life" implying that all life—no matter what shape, condition, environment, or importance—must be preserved. My stand is somewhat in the middle. All that can be said here is that as we walk the grey area between life and death, the usual distinctions do not help in making decisions. In this grey area we stand many times in a particular situation which is not covered by our general ideals and principles because no general statement can cover all particular realities. We act and accept the responsibility of our actions before God and our fellowman.

Aside from the medical staff, the hospital chaplain or pastor often becomes a member of the community surrounding the terminally ill patient. He will be as effective as is his ability to face the reality of his own death and to be able to listen to the emotions of others. He is a special representative of the Church in this situation.

He must not be afraid to pray. This may seem a senseless suggestion. But many ministers and priests, lacking confidence in prayer, impose their lack of confidence upon those they serve. He must not be afraid of God and the Christian values of his denomination. Sick people want to hear about these values and about God. At the same time he must not sermonize. First comes honest concern for this sick person. Part of this honest concern is providing an occasion for the sick person to speak of and pray to God. Sometimes he or she may not wish to do this at all. If the chaplain is experienced in the ways of the sick, he can be very helpful throughout the dying process by facilitating communication between the members of the sickness-community. Suffering, both physical and psychological, is a heavy burden to bear, but the chaplain can make the yoke lighter by offering the faith of the Church and his experience of dealing with people. More will be said about his role in the total sickness situation in the theological reflections which follow.

The Church's preparation of its members for death begins while they are alive. Death must be spoken of from the pulpit. Not in the fire and brimstone images of the past, nor in the often complete agnosticism of the present, but rather in the covenant-awareness of perennial Christianity. If the priest or minister cannot be at ease with death, who can be? We need sermons on death.

When death occurs, it is important that the pastor give warm, personal support. He can be of great help in planning the funeral. Especially when there has not been any preplanning, he can be on hand to help the survivors—who usually are prone to great extravagance in funeral arrangements. The warmth and solidarity felt with the pastor can do more to relieve the sense of guilt experienced at this time than can the expenditures of large sums of money.

A funeral service reflects the values of the community. How the body is honored, how much money is spent, the consideration given to the enduring qualities of the deceased—all the various elements of the funeral reflect the values of the community. Can a pastor allow the ritual action of the funeral to give lie to the beliefs of the Church? To help the ritual truly portray Christian beliefs, he should give great care to everything connected with the funeral and the funeral preparations.

In contemporary films and novels, funeral directors are painted as money-hungry, weird, and not-too-human individuals. As death nears, the prospect of encountering some of these imaginary creatures looms large on the horizon. Ideally, provisions for a funeral are taken care of before death, but many times the survivors are making the preparations just before or after death. Burdened by the tension of a long illness or of a sudden terrible death they go about their business of contacting a funeral director.

Most directors are not bad men. They have been the object of unkind criticism because of their tendency to encourage ostentatious and extravagant funerals. More will be said about funerals in the following chapter. Here I would only mention that plans should be made before the death. To make them at death is to leave oneself open to all the pressures of buying in a critical situation.

Funeral directors, hospital staff, friends . . . so many people surround the dying—sometimes! Dying shares the loneliness of living. A lot of people die alone. No one knows their death or mourns their passing life. Like apples, old and rotten, they fall to the ground and are forgotten. Dying is human when the community with whom the individual has shared life is present to share death. Dying is animal when the community does not know life has passed out of it.

Suggestions for Personal Reflection:

1. Are you afraid of a prolonged illness and suffering?
2. Would you want to be told that you are about to die?
3. How do you react to crises? How did you feel when you were married? At your last serious illness? At the death or near-death of someone close to you?
4. Do you find it easy to express your deep feelings to those very close to you?

Suggestions for Group Reflection:

1. Should a person be told that he is going to die?
2. Could you let someone die while knowing that an extremely expensive operation might let him live a little longer?
3. What has been your experience with hospital chaplains? Funeral directors?

CHAPTER III—SICKNESS, DYING AND THE CHURCH

"This prayer, made in faith, will heal the sick man; the Lord will restore him to health, and the sins he has committed will be forgiven. So then, confess your sins to one another, and pray for one another so that you will be healed. The prayer of a good man has a powerful effect."

James 5:15-16

Within the illness situation we still live, breathe, and react as human beings. And, as with anything human, there is a further meaning to what occurs. Just as the significance of this illness changes if the patient is spouse, mother, father, child, or distant friend, so too an added dimension of the illness can be understood if the patient is Christian. To understand the fullness of everyone's role in this situation, I must speak of the Church as a healing church.[1]

To say that the Church heals may sound strange. To say that the Church is "a healing church" may recall the emotion of the faith-healer. Yet if we pause and reflect upon what healing is, we can see that this is a beautiful title for the Church. The theologian Paul Tillich describes healing as the means of reuniting that which is estranged, giving a center to that which is split, overcoming the split between God and man, man and his world, man and himself. Put in another way, healing is complete when a man is full of life. This is what the Church's function is on this earth: to overcome the split, to bring life.

The Second Vatican Council declared, "By her relationship with Christ, the Church is a kind of sacrament or sign of intimate union with God, and of the unity of all mankind. She is also an instrument for the achievement of such union and unity" (Constitution on the Church, #1). This is an excellent way of stating that the Church, as such, is a sign and instrument of the reunion of the estranged, of the healing of that split between God and man, man and the world, man and himself.

The Church which is the healing sacrament is ourselves, the people of God. As Christ's body on earth, we extend His presence in our communal activities and in our individual lives. We, as church, are the source of life and the center of that which is split. We are the sacrament of Christ's presence to the world. We are the healing Church.

The concept of the Church as ourselves, as body of Christ, as people of God, etc., is well known as a result of the writings of modern theologians. But do we also see the Church as a sign and an instrument of the healing of the split *within ourselves*? And even more do we also see it as the sacrament of healing the split present within those of us who are sick? For in sickness there is a division between our desire and God's desire (that we be a whole human being, a human being capable of fulfilling our divine vocation) and the actual disease-ridden state of our bodies. There is a split between what was called in Greek categories "body" and "soul." We easily acknowledge the fact that the doctor, the nurses, the pharmacist, and even the nurse's aide have a role in healing the split in the patient. Yet there is at times a difficulty in seeing that the Church too has a role in healing. How strange! One reason for the difficulty in accepting the Church's role in the sickness situation may be the result of our former categories of "body" and "soul." We have been brought up to think that the Church is to care for our *soul*, while secular institutions are to care for our *body*.

In what follows it is important to realize that we speak in terms of man as a totality. Man is *one*. What affects man's spirit affects his body; what affects the body affects the spirit. A brief reflection upon our own bouts with sickness shows this. A headache, a warm room, an operation—all these affect our conscious relationship to God and others.

The Church has a role in healing the sick. She continues the mission of Christ on earth to preach and heal the sick. Christ gave that mission to His church. And this same Church continues the mission to this very day through the hands of her individual members and the "hands" of the community: the sacraments.

Christ's mission in life and death was to heal man. His mission was to bring man to the fullness of life through association with His personhood. Notice that in His healing ministry Jesus Christ always demands a faith which is directed to the coming of His kingdom. It is a faith which includes total confidence in His own person (Mt 9:22, 15:28, Mk 10:52). His various cures are symbolic (in the full sense of the word) of the destruction of the kingdom of evil and the advancement of the reign of God. Christ's mission is forcibly brought out in His answer to John's disciples. "See," He said, "the blind receive their sight and the lame walk, lepers are cleansed and the deaf hear, and the dead are raised up, and the poor have the good news preached to them" (Mt 11:4-5). This was His mission. Day in and day out, He traveled the country healing the sick in mind and body, preaching the good news that the division between God and man was at an end. Man had a new life.

Christ daily performed miracles to conquer the evil in the world and establish the kingdom of God. With spittle, clay, a gentle touch of the hand, He healed. The miracles were His way of bringing salvation to the world. Salvation, as God's invitation to man to live together with Him, had to be manifest in earthly realities if enfleshed man were to respond to God. Salvation is first of all present in the person of Christ, and secondly in the actions of Christ which specify how God is saving man. Christ came to save man as man is—a unity of body and spirit. The miracles of Christ did this, for they dealt with man not only as a body that was sick, but also as a person that needed salvation from evil. Yet not only were Christ's miracles concerned with the sick present before Him; they looked forward to that day when the new man in his resurrected body would have the fullness of life. A miracle has been described as the entrance of God into our lives when we can no longer help ourselves. This is why Christ came: to enable man to become whole, to reconcile the split in man between God and man, man and the other men, and man with himself. He did this through His miracles on this earth. He did this especially through His death and resurrection. Man could never do this himself.

It was in Christ's death and resurrection that the miracle of reconciliation was achieved. Christ in His death encountered and overcame the ground of all evil. He saw evil and overcame it. He met pain, suffering, and isolation and, through the wonderful law of the Cross, saw His pain, His suffering, and His isolation converted by His Father into His glorious resurrection (Rom 5). As a result of Christ's death and resurrection, mankind now knew that it would live forever.

The Church resulted from Christ's paschal mystery. Like Christ, the Church had the mission to heal and to preach. In the Gospel, we hear Christ send His apostles forth to preach the word and to heal the sick (cf. Mt

10:1 ff; Mk 16:17-18). The record of the early Church, as contained in the Acts of the Apostles, shows the apostles performing that mission (cf. Acts 3; 5:12 ff; 8:7; 9:32 ff; 14:8 ff; 28:8 ff). Peter and Paul carry the Church from Jerusalem to the world. They preach, they heal, they continue the mission of Christ to save the whole man. They are not the only ones, of course, to enjoy the power of healing. Rather, this is a gift present in the whole Church. It is one of the gifts which Paul mentions as being distributed by the Spirit within the Church (cf. 1 Cor 12).

The Letter of James has always been the Church's favorite reading for sickness. In the fifth chapter, we hear James tell the Christians what to do when they are sick. They shall call in the "presbyter." They shall pray over the sick person and anoint him with oil in the name of the Lord. As a result of their faithful prayers, he shall be raised up; his sins will be forgiven him.

It is no wonder that this has been a favorite citation of the Church. In this quotation, the apostle James reminds us that the Church is to pray for the sick. The Church is to bring the sacraments to the sick. And, in particular, the anointing of the sick is to be the Church's special way of bringing salvation to them.

In the depths of serious sickness, the Church is to make Christ present once again. Christ present in His Church, through oil, words, and the action of anointing, touches the sick person to give him life.

The use of anointing for health and not for death is a point that must be emphasized. It allows one to read St. James with clear vision, and to understand why anointing is not celebrated with those in proximate danger of death from causes other than sickness—criminals about to be executed, soldiers going to battle, etc.

It is the only view which clears away the theological dead wood that has surrounded the anointing with oil since the 13th century. It is also a common ground between the denominations.

When one looks at the history of anointing, it can be seen that understanding it as the sacrament of "extreme unction" is certainly an overemphasis against the stronger (nearly 1,000 years) tradition of anointing as a sacrament of the sick. Until the 13th century there were tremendous variations in the methods of anointing, times of anointing, conditions of the patient anointed. The sick were anointed at the spot of greatest pain, or on all the extremities; at times they even drank the oil. Some Spanish rituals mention the fact that the people were anointed on seven successive days of their illness, or until they got better. The condition required for anointing was that a person be judged seriously ill. Such a judgment was to be made by those who were to officiate at the celebration of the sacrament. It was only natural that some of these people who were anointed would be at the point of death. After the 10th century, a development in the practice and theology of the anointing occurs. Because of the high "stole-fees"[2] and because of the necessity of receiving penance before anointing, the anointing of the sick became associated with the rites celebrated at death. Scholastic theologians reflected upon the sacrament as they knew it—as "extreme unction." These men, in addition, found it difficult to see a sacrament as beneficial to the body. All these factors combined to present us with the situation as we find it today where some Christians associate anointing with death, not with life.

This brief excursus was necessary to understand why anointing of the sick can and must be seen as the extension of the Father's salvation to us through

Christ's anointing of the sick. For salvation is being offered to this sick person at a critical situation in his life. Christ is present offering the individual an opportunity to enter into His Passover, which brings life to the entire person.

Christ comes to the sick not only in the anointing of the sick but in all His sacraments. He is there to help us, to unite His strength with ours so that we may live. Christ comes to us to join us to His paschal mystery. He leads us through suffering to the final resurrection.

We are involved with the mission of the Church when we are sick or when we are caring for the sick. Many times when we are filled with the isolated pain and bone-filled suffering of sickness, we fail to sense this involvement. A hospital is a place surrounded with large signs stating "Silence, Please!" and filled with people saying "Sh-h-h, he needs rest." This gives us the impression that the hospital or sick room is a place separate from the world, separate from the mission of the Church. We forget where the action was for Christ —on the Cross. We forget that there is vital activity in the sleep of the exhausted patient. Wherever evil is conquered, there is Christ bringing life, even if this conquering occurs in the quiet action of a sick person.

The sick participate in the Church's mission by fighting the physical evil that is attempting to overwhelm them. They bring to sickness their whole Christian personality. If they have constantly fought the evils they have met in their lives, whether these were physical, social, or moral, they enter into sickness with the attitude necessary to continue the Christian mission. They recognize the evil of sickness and strive to overcome it. The weapons provided for this battle are the doctors, nurses, medicines, sacraments, and continual prayer.

A person uses these weapons by cooperating with the

medical experts and by growth in the life of prayer. It is in private and sacramental prayer that he deepens the bond with Christ, the source of all life. Prayer is basically the prayer of Christ: "Father, not my will but yours be done." What the individual seeks is the Father's will. But this is not a will demanding passive acceptance of all that happens around him. The will of the Father is the source of life for all. The sick know that no matter what happens, it is this full life that is given to them. It is a person's disposition of happiness in doing the Father's will that enables him to further the mission of Christ. For in the acceptance of God's will he becomes a true source of grace for others. The sick, like Christ on the Cross, change suffering and pain into grace and life for others, especially for those who are near them. This disposition of happiness also has an effect upon the whole person in providing the necessary dispositions for full health.

Caring for the sick is a real service of the Church—not only of the Church as present in the ordained, but also the Church as present in each of the baptized. It is a real gift and favor of God to be able to care for the sick. It is through people who have the gift of healing that other people will be healed. We are all familiar with the nurse, doctor, or aide who is as cold and sharp as some of the needles he or she pokes into us. We recognize the difference between these kinds of people and those who see their work as a genuine loving service to whole persons instead of bodies. Aside from those directly associated with sickness in a professional manner, many ordinary women and men spend their time with the sick. They may be mothers, husbands, wives. No matter who they are, they too participate in the mission of the Church to heal the sick. Their patience, love, and—ultimately—merely their presence continue Christ's mission to the sick of the world. All of us can help in some way.

Whenever someone who is sick is restored to the risen life of Christ through the victory of the Cross, whenever Christ once again touches the sick to bring them to salvation, there the healing Church *is* no matter what the outward and visible results of her healing may be. Especially in the anointing of the sick, the priest or minister as the special representative of the Church heals the sick. In it, Christ is present in a special way, saying once again that the lame walk, the blind see, and the sick are healed.

The relationship of the sick person to ourselves or ourselves to the sick person involves a concept of representation. When we speak of one who represents the community we think usually of someone who does something "for" the community or who acts "instead of" the community. This view is not entirely correct. If we look at Christ who was *the* representative of man, we can see the perfect example of what "representation" is. In His life, death, and resurrection, Christ was not someone separate from the community of mankind; what happened to Christ affected mankind as a whole. Christ was mankind in some mysterious way. In other words, He did not act so much for the community or instead of the community; He *was* the community acting.

As with Christ, so too with individual Christians and the Christian community. The principle of representation is applicable among them too. Anyone who takes seriously Christ's concept of "neighbor" must see the individual as a basic representative of Christ, and in turn of the Christian community (cf. Mt 10:14 ff; 18:5; Lk 10:16; Jn 13:30; Mt 25). Thus, to apply this principle to the healing situation, it is Christ who heals; it is Christ who is healed.

Christ's actions of healing, preaching, suffering, and rising were true signs of His election by the Father. One who has entered into the risen Christ through the rite of initiation has entered into this election. Thus it can be said that the healing, preaching, suffering, and gradual growth in the life of the resurrection are at one and the same time both a means of assuming this life's election and a demonstration of one's election. A sick person is therefore selected as a representative of the Church and of Christ in his sickness.

Thus we can say that we are related to the sick person and the sick person to us in two ways: 1) The individual is representative of the resurrected Christ conquering evil and extending the kingdom. 2) We, as the community, are Christ extending Himself in time and offering a further entrance into the mystery of His Passover. These relationships call for specific attitudes on the part of both the patient and the community.

The patient should understand his representative role. It is not passive. As a representative of the community, his attitude should be one of acceptance of his role in the community and a willingness to accept this burden. His task is to overcome sickness and to further the kingdom by getting better. The conquering of sickness is not only a cure of the body through the use of pills and surgery—although this is one aspect of overcoming sickness. One conquers the evil of sickness by bringing together the split between man and God, man and man, man and himself. This does not always necessitate the here and now bodily healing of a person, just as the bodily healing of a person does not always signify the advancement of the kingdom. Health must be seen more in the light of the total vocation of man.

Health is that state in which man is able to respond

to the call of God with the fullness of his being. Our healing act (whether as patient or community) *must* be a participation in the action of the one who is the divine physician: Jesus Christ who has gone to the Father, thus uniting us to God; who enjoys the fullness of His resurrection, thus is united in body; and who is constantly bringing all men into unity with each other through His Church.

When a person is sick with a terminal illness, he still participates in the Church as a healing community. His hope is founded in Jesus, who continues to conquer the evil of sickness through him. In the patient's recognition that death is not absurd, that it is not the end of all, that it is in reality a part of life—in these he conquers the sting of death. He knows with each celebration of eucharist that he enters more deeply into his baptismal promise. He knows that with the last breath his baptism is fulfilled: He has died with Christ and rises with Christ. Never to die again!

Suggestions for Personal Reflection:

1. Do you think praying for the sick is worthwhile?
2. Visit the hospital. Talk with someone who is ill. Write down some of your reflections.
3. Read Jn 5:1-19; chapter 9; Mk chapter 2.

Suggestions for Group Reflection:

1. Is there any use in praying for the sick?
2. What do you think about suffering?
3. Everyone should bring the name and story of one sick person to the group. The group should pray for each of the persons mentioned.

CHAPTER IV—THE LIVING AND THE DEAD

"She looks so nice."

"Our Father who art in heaven . . ."

"Funerals are morbid."

". . . hallowed be thy name. Thy kingdom come."

"Henry, Billy is pulling her hair again. Put him over here!"

". . . thy will be done on earth as it is in heaven."

"I'm sorry to hear she died. She was a good woman."

"Give us this day our daily bread . . . and forgive us our trespasses . . ."

Bits of conversation, bits of life, snatches of prayer—slowly the mosaic of mourning the dead is pieced together to offer the living a fuller life. Once a person dies, his memory continues on. But once a person dies, those whose lives have been in turmoil must now attain a forward motion of life. They must pull themselves out of the vortex of death into the forwardness of life.

This is not easy. Nor must death be faced alone. A mourning ritual has developed in most societies to provide a context of individual grieving and communal support for the bereaved.

To live fruitfully after the death of a loved one, a person must go through a period of mourning. One of the most important studies on mourning is a paper by Dr. Erich Lindemann of Harvard entitled "Symptomatology and Management of Acute Grief."[1] Another popular presentation is by E. James Lieberman entitled "Americans No Longer Know How to Mourn."[2]

What Dr. Lindemann found in comparing the mourners and nonmourners has come to be considered the classic syndrome of bereavement. Normal grief includes waves of somatic distress lasting from twenty minutes to an hour; a tightness in the throat; frequent crying and sighing; a feeling of emptiness, weakness, and tension; a sense of heaviness, fatigue, and a lack of appetite; a preoccupation with death and the deceased; a distance from and a loss of warmth for other people, including a tendency to respond with irritation and anger and to handle others in a stiff, formal manner; much talking about the deceased.

"The bereaved," he writes, "is surprised to find how large a part of his customary activity was done in some meaningful relationship to the deceased and how it has now lost its significance." He says that grieving persons often reflect some of the traits of the deceased during these days of mourning. Significantly, Dr. Lindemann finds that if the mourner lets himself experience his grief he can deal emotionally with the experience of loss in from four to six weeks. It is during this time that a rapid relief of tension is also experienced.

But what happens if a survivor does not go through the grieving process? A great deal. Psychiatric literature is full of cases of severe emotional upset caused by failure to grieve properly. The survivor will almost assuredly have emotional problems in his relationship to other people if he does not grieve properly. He cannot invest emotional energy in living until he has withdrawn it from the deceased.

The experience of Dr. Lieberman and others bears this out. A middle-aged man loses his wife, upon whom he was very dependent. No tears, but a paranoid psychosis. . . . A woman whose father commits suicide can never fully grieve—whether due to anger or guilt—and spends years searching hopelessly for some kind of replacement in another man. . . . A young mother loses a child, and the next one is forced into the role of inadequate substitute. . . . Most clinicians nowadays will regard the failure to cry at the funeral of a loved one as a sign of blocked grief. The failure to attend a funeral, not caring where the grave is, etc., would indicate a more abnormal reaction. This is not to say that a funeral service is necessary for a full mourning process. A memorial service, for instance, fulfills the same function.

All intimate relationships have some ambivalence.[3] The ability to grieve means essentially that hate and love can be faced, weighed, worked through, and thus integrated, rather than allowed to hover tensely beneath the surface for years.

Our society in general is not comfortable with grief. It shuns it. Many adults are afraid to let their children see them weep. So the children believe that crying, even over death, is immature; a loss of self-control; a threat to order, objectivity, intellect, and morale. Undoubtedly, much of the unemotionalism is a product of this country's Anglo-Saxon-Teutonic heritage, the heritage of the stiff upper lip, of "bearing up, old chap."

Unemotionalism is characteristic of this overpopulated world in which people hide their emotions as their forefathers hid their money. Now the money (as a sign of power) is more likely to be visible and the emotions (a sign of weakness) hidden. There is a new, keener sense of territorial imperative in a world that seems so unstable and ever shrinking, and the territory that is to be sealed off includes the emotions.

Anger is one emotion that is part of grief. But revenge, remorse, regret are all anti-grief, dead-end emotions. Anger at a death without meaning is understandable; but that anger should not be allowed to degenerate into cynicism, depression, or destructiveness. Constructively used, anger can purchase a meaning for death. As an extreme example, a person who is angry because his wife dies of cancer can try to conquer the disease through personal research, or monetary support of others' research.

People seem not so much to fear death as to fear a meaningless death. Modern society can guarantee painless death and perhaps even stave it off for a while, but it cannot guarantee a meaningful death. Meanings are not for sale. Meanings give joy, but cost grief.

The theory of "grief work" is basically an optimistic one: If a bereaved person goes through grief fully, he can emerge from an important loss a whole person. "Better to have loved and lost than never to have loved at all."

How does a person undergo "normal grief"?

Some people seem to be in favor of getting emotions out into the open in a simple wholesale purge. This approach may polarize the bleeding hearts against the stout hearts because it seems to justify everything from temper tantrums to sackcloth and ashes.

It is not the volume of tears but the content of emotion that matters: the meaning, the awful necessity of letting go of what no longer exists except in memories. Crying for its own sake is no better than taking out aggression on a punching bag—both are probably irrelevant, although they may produce better boxers and actresses. The emotions, to be meaningful, must be focused on something real. Hysteria and chaotic loss of control never helped anyone and are not necessarily better than stony-faced emotional paralysis (their opposite). Like tantrums, vis-a-vis anger, hysterical mourning is only a parody of normal grief. Such overreactions, while sometimes quite understandable, are not to be encouraged. On the other hand, failure to weep for a loved one is usually a sign of an emotional block that will take its toll in the future.

The emotions of grieving tend to cluster about three main psychological processes: identification, substitution, and feelings of guilt.[4] Within bounds, each is a normal and a valid expression of the deep feelings of the individual which can be worked through and resolved. When the expression is delayed or repressed, it tends to find its outlet in less desirable forms.

In identification, the one who is grieving identifies his feelings and, at times, even himself with the deceased. "Dad wouldn't want me to cry," he says. And consequently he acts as "Dad," the deceased, would act. Temporary identification with the deceased can be expected. There are cases where the identity of the bereaved and the deceased become permanent, for instance when the bereaved acquires the symptoms of the deceased's illness. If he cannot shake such an identification he may become seriously ill. Some identification with the ideals and life of the deceased is healthy and necessary; too much is disastrous.

Substitution is somewhat similar. In this instance the bereaved is overwhelmed by the loss of the deceased. To cope with this loss he substitutes something identified with the person for the person himself. Not knowing what to do with the former emotions he had toward the deceased, he attaches these emotions to something else. Thus the cemetery plot, a picture, his room become substitutes for the deceased. On a temporary basis, this can serve a useful purpose while the bereaved is withdrawing his emotional investment from the past and preparing to reinvest it in the future. Memorial funds of all sorts are a result of this emotion of grief. Walking through Harvard recently I was struck by how many buildings were built in honor of the dead: the campus was composed of these headstones built to honor the dead.

In acute grief, the element of guilt is invariably present. This is probably due to the ambivalent quality in the love relationship where there is self-giving and self-satisfying, a craving for mutuality between loved and lover, as well as the resentment of loss of freedom. When the object of love disappears, the feelings are set free and guilt enters. The guilt may be expressed in excessive idealizing of the deceased, or in feelings expressed in such phrases as, "If I had only known . . ." "If I had it to do over again . . ." "Why did I fail to do . . ." Such self-condemnation is a normal part of the process of emotional withdrawal. However, if it is more an expression of low self-esteem than of normal grief, it may precipitate a period of depression and melancholia with all of the irrational and excessive feelings that accompany it.

As can be seen, each of the emotions associated with grief can be the result of either a normal or an abnormal reaction to the situation. This is only to say that our entire person is involved in death. Memories, emotions, hopes, thoughts—*every part of us* reacts when death enters into our lives. Death is such an overwhelming and radical part of our individual and social life that every society has developed rituals to cope with its trauma.

The rituals may be strictly religious, strictly secular, or—as is usually the case—a mixture of both. The "Irish wake" has become famous; yet essentially it is a way this ethnic group copes with death.

The book *La Guerre, Yes Sir!*[5] brings out forcefully the contrast in mourning ritual of two cultures: English and French Canadian. In flawless imagery Roch Carrier presents the English soldiers with stiff upper lips standing at attention at the coffin of a French Canadian soldier. The English gaze upon the French Canadian mourning: singing, dancing, drinking, laughing, praying, fighting—they see a disgrace to the dead. The French, on the other hand, see the English as cold, unfeeling, ignorant of this man's life as well as his death. Two cultures face to face over the same death. Each involved in a meaningful ritual; yet each unable to communicate to the other.

Anger, identification, substitution, guilt—all these emotions are expressed within every culture. They are part of the mosaic of mourning which is for the living and the dead.

Suggestions for Personal Reflection:

1. Is there anyone you have known in your life for whom you have not grieved?
2. For what in your life would you wish to be remembered?
3. If someone close to you (husband/wife/parent/child) were about to die, is there anything you would wish you had done for him or her?
4. Compose a prayer to be said at the graves of three people you love a great deal.
5. Can you remember how you felt when you had to receive condolences from others?

Suggestions for Group Reflection:

1. Do you find it easy to distinguish between what you feel and what you think?
2. Do you think it necessary to express your grief?
3. Quiet reflection and verbal prayer for a dead person.

57

CHAPTER V
—THE LIVING, THE DEAD AND THE CHURCH

"If we have died with Christ, we believe that we will also live with him."

(Rom 6:8)

We in North America frequently look upon rituals as stark, lifeless, without meaning. This may be because many of the rituals we have been exposed to are mere remnants of a colorful, vital, and meaningful past. They do not speak to the present. A true ritual has the ability to reinvoke past emotion, to bind the individual to his own past experience, and to bring the members of the group together in a shared experience. A ritual, though essentially repetitious, is able to express and constructively channelize the reactions of the mourners. The individual should be able to find his own emotions, thoughts, doubts, and convictions resonating within the ritual. The community, on the other hand, should find its deep-felt grief and desire to help engrained in the ritual action. A ritual does not destroy the personal. Nor does it take away freedom. Rather, it provides a context within which the personal feelings of all the mourners can be expressed, and it offers each individual the occasion to support freely every other individual in this time of crisis.

The Christian community has its rituals. They reflect Christian man's awareness of the mystery of life. Just as man differs throughout the world and throughout history, so his rituals differ. Yet since Christianity does have a shared belief, there are also common elements which reflect her history and peoples. The reality of death and the hope of a new life have been constant meanings in the Christian ritual of death. Scripture reading, songs, and prayers for the dead have been constant ways through which these meanings have been expressed. The community's liturgical celebration of these "constants" has varied and has usually swung from one external expression to another.

The liturgical reform presently sweeping Christian denominations places most of us in the "in-between times" of being raised in one liturgy and celebrating in another. In the churches with a strong liturgical tradition, the change is most evident in the colors and music used at the wake, church service, and burial. Black vestments and sober dress have given way to white vestments and joyful celebration.

The former ritual expressed the medieval concern with the terror and fear of death. The Black Plague seemed to hang over the wake, church service, and burial. In the Roman liturgy, for instance, black vestments, incense, and Latin chant filled the senses with the foreboding of Dante's inferno rather than with joy of the resurrection. When a person died, gloom and doom were the order of the day. The solemn and booming tones of the preacher's sermon reminded us in word what the Roman liturgy decreed in action: Man is a sinful creature composed of a body which pulls him to evil earth and a soul which is made for God Himself. The prayers pleaded for mercy, escape from the judgment of condemnation and the wrath to come on that "final" day. An individual brought up on this liturgy and concept of death will be amazed at the new rites that he encounters. Formed by the former funeral ritual, he may feel that the new one is empty, fearful of facing the realities of death, and forgetful of man's sinfulness. At the same time he may appreciate the new rites for what they do express.

The theme of hope and resurrection predominates in

many of the new funeral rites. A more reflective consideration of hope will be taken up in the final chapter. Here we are looking at what the complex of ritual should express and how it may accomplish this goal. It is difficult to "talk" about ritual. To understand ritual, one must participate in it. It is also difficult to understand a ritual if one does not believe its fundamental presuppositions. Without faith a ritual is lifeless, without meaning. It is shadows that never become enfleshed, reflected on church floors. Because of these difficulties, our discussion here can only hint at the reality. Yet it is within these rituals that the living encounter the memories and realities of the dead so that both may live in peace.

There are many books and articles suggesting what to do at the wake, church service, and burial. Each Christian community has its own tradition. In the majority of cases, the minister or priest will use the approved ritual of his denomination. In the majority of cases, too, everyone will be pleased with what is presented. What follows will probably agree with some of the ritual and disagree with others as found in the respective denominations. At the same time it does reflect the constant tradition of the Christian church.

Whether it is a memorial service or the wake, church service, and burial liturgy, the ritual must provide an opportunity for the following:[1]

Regeneration, in which the deceased lives again in the memory of all present and an opportunity is provided for all present to face up to their past, present, and future relationship to the deceased.

Identification, in which the survivors recognize their share in the life of the deceased and their responsibility for guarding the values for which he lived. It is here, too, that people are given the opportunity to see that it is by their identification with these values that they will immortalize him. On one occasion I had the opportunity to participate in a eucharistic celebration for the dead where everyone came in great sorrow and left with great joy. A husband, the father of seven children, had died. The wife gave the homily in such a way that all of us present could only share her strength and reach for her husband's values. Each person has a unique personality, whether child or adult. The ritual should provide the opportunity for us to identify with the values of that person.

Communal awareness comes in a recognition that by the death of the deceased they have become a new community. When one of our friends dies, we are not the same. This change must be recognized. Whenever a prime minister or president dies in office the nation recognizes it is not the same. A husband's or wife's death immediately affects the entire family. But what holds for nation or family also holds for the less formal communities of sport, work, Church, etc. The survivors are not quite the same people as they once were. Each must reestablish his relationship with the others. The rite should provide the opportunity for all to come and do this.

Confirmation of communal values which form the foundation of everyone's belief. In this Christian community, the particular themes of the reality of death and the hope of resurrection should be found in the liturgy. The deep meaning of life and death must be affirmed here. People want to hear from those knowledgeable and experienced about life's meaning and death's hope. They should not be handed stones instead of bread.

Finding a suitable outlet for identification, substitution, and guilt. All of these will have a suitable outlet if the rite provides for the three above-mentioned elements. The purpose of the rite is to provide everyone an opportunity for emotional release and community awareness. It does this through remembering the deceased both as a valuable person and as an important member of the community. It looks with the eyes of faith and sees the Spirit working through him and the community for the upbuilding of the world. It says "Amen" to what was and "Maranatha" (Come, Lord Jesus!) to what will be.

A number of Christian denominations divide the death liturgy into the wake, church service, and burial.

The purpose of the *wake* is to allow individuals to come to terms with the dead, to help them to accept not only his life for what it was, but to begin to accept the finality, in human terms, of death. Here is an opportunity for regeneration and identification. People should be allowed to relax and to have the opportunity to reflect quietly about the meaning of the deceased's life in relation to the community and to themselves. The Scripture readings, the silence, the song, the materials used should all focus upon this one purpose. For instance, after some readings, prayer, song, and silence, everyone may share a personal incident involving the deceased. The tone of the sharing will determine how the wake should end. Perhaps a corporate expression of sorrow and a prayer for absolution would be an appropriate ending.

The mood of the wake should not be that of people without a meaning, but it should be joyful. Not the joy of hollow laughter down empty halls but rather the joy of knowing that someone we love is free and happy.

The *church service* should attempt to focus upon the principal themes of death and hope. In the early Church, it was the death itself of the Christian which was celebrated. The custom of having a eucharistic celebration during the funeral or with the body present is never referred to before the seventh century and was a regular practice only after the 13th.

This historical fact is mentioned to show that the growing practice of memorial services is similar in many respects to that of the early Church, and to emphasize that the church service should not concentrate on the body of the deceased but upon the communal values and the reality of this person's death. Perhaps a short description of one rite would be helpful. The following is from the Roman Catholic tradition.

The priest greets the body, relatives, and close friends of the deceased at the door of the church. The box or casket is covered with a cloth of appropriate color. As in our baptism when the priest meets us at the same door and inquires what we ask of the Church, to which we respond, "Faith," here too at the consummation of a faith-filled life, all present implicitly ask for faith.

Lighter colors are used to indicate the joy of this person's new life. The paschal candle (the large decorated candle that stands beside the altar from Easter to Ascension Thursday) stands near the coffin to emphasize the link between the individual's baptism, where he died with Christ, and his promised resurrection with this same Christ. There is the custom too, of placing the body of the deceased person in the traditional position of the liturgical celebration: the faithful facing the altar and the clergy facing the people.

A reverence (bow) is usually made to the body. This is to acknowledge the fact that this indeed is a holy place.

There are many prayers that the priest may choose from for the service. But notice these two prayers:

Lord God, Almighty Father, our faith testifies that your Son died for us and rose to life again. May our brother (sister), N., share in this mystery: as he (she) has gone to his (her) rest believing in Jesus, may he (she) share through Him the joy of the resurrection. We ask this through Christ our Lord.   Amen.

For a married couple:

Lord, pardon the sins of your servants, N. and N. In this life you brought them together in true married love. Grant that now they may live in the fullness of eternal love forever. We ask this through Christ our Lord.   Amen.

The sermon (homily) should not be a funeral eulogy, according to the directions specified for the priest. However, sometimes a funeral eulogy will be given, for, unfortunately, most people are accustomed to it. They are not accustomed to what is required: a proclamation of the good news of resurrection life.

After the homily, the community prays the prayer of the faithful. This is a prayer which reflects both the universal needs of the Church and the particular needs of the community. It is an appropriate place for spontaneous prayers from all present.

The preparation of the altar is an opportunity not only to bring the gifts of bread and wine to the altar but also to bring those products of the deceased's gifts to the world. An object that is an expression of his life should also be brought to the altar: a favorite book, pipe, hammer, ring of keys, glasses, old hat, etc.

The eucharistic celebration is always a celebration of life. One's baptismal life and death are celebrated when we once again "do this in memory." We take, bless, break, and share the Lord's body and blood. We become one with Him and each other. We who eat and drink this bread and wine shall have eternal life. Once again we are joined to the one who has recently died. Through the signs of bread and wine, we are joined to Christ and the deceased. He is really alive. He is actually joined with us in this earthly celebration of the eternal sacrament of Jesus Christ. We look forward to the time when sacraments are no longer necessary, when we can be with the deceased face to face and not through signs. We look forward to the day when we can once again be together. But until then it is the union in sign, through bread and wine, that we become one body with Christ and each other.

In eucharist there is also forgiveness of sins. With the eucharist there should be an end to the reasons for guilt. As Christ said, "Forgive them for they know not what they do," so one can be sure that as the deceased is one with Christ in the happiness of His resurrection, so he is one with Him in His forgiveness. And He forgives all.

The church service ends with a short commendation and farewell which might be along the following lines:
Our prayers are ended, and now we bid our last
farewell.
There is sadness in the parting, but yet it
should fill us with new hope,
for one day we shall see our brother (sister)
again and enjoy his (her) love.
By God's mercy, we who leave this church today
in sorrow will be reunited in God's kingdom.
Let us comfort one another in the faith of Jesus
Christ.
or
Before we go our separate ways, let us take
leave of our brother (sister).
May this last farewell express the depth of our

love for him (her),
ease our sadness, and strengthen our hope.
We know that one day we shall joyfully
embrace him (her) once again
where the love of Christ, which overcomes all
things, will destroy
even death itself.

The *burial service,* if there is one, confronts survivors with the grave. It is especially at this point that they must let go of the dead, for here it is evident that they must go on living without this person, yet living in light of the resurrection. With the burial, the living walk away. As the one who has died has changed, so have they. The living will never be the same. One is missing from their midst. But this is the fate of every man: to miss those we love; to feel the sting of death even while we live.

Suggestions for Personal Reflection:

Read, reflect, and note some of your ideas from the readings in Appendix "A."

Suggestions for Group Reflection:

1. What are some rituals in your personal life that you have found useful?
2. Would you want a church service at your funeral? Why?
3. What would you tell a child about death?

CHAPTER VI—PREPARING THE CHILDREN

The animal runs, it passes, it dies.
And it is the great cold.
It is the great cold of the night, it is the dark.

The bird flies, it passes, it dies.
And it is the great cold.
It is the great cold of the night, it is the dark.

The fish flees, it passes, it dies.
And it is the great cold.
It is the great cold of the night, it is the dark.

Man eats and sleeps. He dies.
And it is the great cold.
It is the great cold of the night, it is the dark.

There is light in the sky, the eyes are extinguished,
the star shines.
The cold is below, the light is on high.

The man has passed, the shade has vanished,
the prisoner is free!

(Gabon Death Rites)

"What to tell the children?" This is the way the question is usually phrased. Why do we think we must *tell* them anything? Ultimately we must use word of mouth, but the fact of the matter is that the children will learn about death from our attitude toward it. No matter what we say with our mouths the children will know our hearts.

The purpose of these reflections has been to help you understand your concept of death. Through conscious reflection it is hoped that your values will shift toward a freer more honest view of death.

Death is a reality. This is the honest statement and realization. Within a Christian context, at least, it is seen as a sacred moment of ultimate faith and involvement with Jesus, an involvement so deep that new life is the ultimate result.

If this is the reality and the conviction of the community of adults, then the children will not be far behind in absorbing the fundamental attitude. Their expressions and verbalizations may be meager, but what is formed in their being is what they have drunk with their mother's milk. Thus what is important is that the death of the individual should be accepted as a natural part of life, and, secondly, that the child should be given that information which is commensurate with his ability.

Any communication demands both speaker and listener. If the child asks a question about death, we must be sure to hear the question, not just the words. He speaks from his background, his fund of experience and his own knowledge. We have to listen to his question. And our response, once we hear the real question, must be within the understanding and experience of the child.

To assist you in this task I would offer the following psychological and theological considerations.[1]

Basic to an understanding of the child is the realization that death is not only a state but a complex symbol, the significance of which will vary from child to child and culture to culture. In addition, the concept of death is very much dependent upon the nature of the developmental process. For convenience sake I shall divide the child's development into three age groupings: three-to-five years, five-to-nine years, nine-to-ten years.

A child under five years of age usually does not recognize death as an irreversible fact. He just does not know death as such. In death, he sees life. He attributes life and consciousness to the dead. For instance, a

four-year-old responded to the question about death: What happens there under the earth?
"He cries because he is dead."
But why should he cry?
"Because he is afraid for himself."[2]
Death is a departure. To die means to live, but under changed circumstances. The sequence of experiencing for the child seems to be that he knows himself as a living being. In his egocentric way he imagines the outside world to be like himself. So in the outside world he imagines everything, including lifeless things and dead people, as alive. Living and lifeless are not yet distinguished in his experience. He extends this animism to death. This does not mean that children have no painful ideas associated with death. In fact, their image of where and how the person lives when they are separated from him is a genuine source of concern. They imagine him as living in the coffin, as feeling pain and sorrow. In particular they imagine death as a very confining situation.

It is within this context that the young child asks questions. We know very little about the after-life. But this is a time in which the reality of a life behind this one is in the child's mind. He thinks in concrete terms. Our response must be in concrete terms. A good example of this can be found in the *Come to the Father* Series for elementary religious education. Their sequence of ideas is as follows for the first grade:[3]

—The title is "Jesus Shows Us the Way to His Father's House."

—The child must become aware of the reality of faith: the joy of having a home where someone who loves us is always waiting for us.

—The instructor is cautioned that sometimes the child may feel an exaggerated fear of death and sometimes he has too materialistic conception of heaven. It is important to gradually dispel these excessive fears and rectify these false notions.

—The instruction should have the following elements:

Yesterday, all of us thought of our home, our home where father and mother always love us and wait for us. Yes, God our Father gives us our home on earth. But this is not all. God our Father loves us so much that he has not only given us a home here but he is also preparing another home for us. He is inviting all of us to his home in heaven. There he wants all of us to be happy with him forever and ever. Yes, all of us here are on our way to God's home in heaven.

One day we will leave our home here where we are already very happy, and go to God's home in heaven where we will be even happier. And we will never have to leave this home, God's home in heaven.

Jesus knows all about this. One day God the Father sent his Son Jesus into the world. Jesus told us his Father's secrets, and then he said to us:

I am going to my Father who is your Father, too. Then Jesus left his home on earth and went to his Father's home in heaven. Heaven is Jesus' home. It is the home of his Father, and that is where Jesus is preparing a place for all of us. In heaven, the home of God our Father, all Jesus' friends are together with God.

Yesterday we heard the Lord Jesus telling us a wonderful secret: God our Father loves us so much that he invites all of us, all the people on earth, to come some day to his home in heaven. There, all of us will be happy with him forever.

We know how our homes on earth are made: they have walls, a roof, stairs; but this is not the most important thing about a home, is it? The most important thing about a home is the happiness of living there together with our father and mother.

God's home in heaven is not made like our homes here. We really don't know how it is made, but then we saw how that was not the most important thing.

What is most important about heaven is living there with God, and with his friends forever.

The second stage, which typifies children between the ages of five and nine, most often sees death as a person and as a real possibility in their life. Death exists but the children still try to keep it distant from themselves. Only those die whom the death-man carries off. Death is an eventuality. Fantasies are also present, though on a less frequent scale, where death and the dead are considered the same. Some of the children consistently use the word death for "the dead." Consequently it might be concluded that they still see death as outside them and not universal. The egocentric, or anthropocentric, view plays a role not only in the birth of animism, but in the formation of artificialism. Every event and change in the world derives from man. If in general death exists, it is a person, the death-man, who "does" it. We get no answer as to why, if death is bad for people, he does it.

If education is a developmental process, if it is a continual exposure of the person to new realities so that he may see the world anew, then the child should be aided in seeing that death is a reality in the world. Perhaps not a person, but nonetheless real—

There are many things in life that are mysterious, that we cannot explain, or that are just too big to be seen entirely. We can't understand them. One thing we do know is that God is bigger than death. He can see all of it. And because He is bigger He can do what

He wants with it. And what He wants is to use it as a way to help us live differently. To allow us to live with Him and everyone else in His home.

Finally, in the third stage (nine-to-ten years), the child begins to recognize death as a process which happens to us according to certain laws. Death is inevitable and universal. As one nine-year-old put it:
What is death? Well, I think it is a part of a
person's life.
Like school. Life has many parts. Only one part
of it is earthly.
As in school, we go to a different class. To die
means to begin
a new life. Everyone has to die once, but the
soul lives on.[4]
A perceptible result of death's process is the dissolution of bodily life. By this time the child knows that death is inevitable. He recognizes it as something he can experience. He sees that its result is a dissolution of bodily life. In this stage, not only does the conception of death become more realistic, but the child's general view of the world veers in this direction. In fact, the child's conception of death reflects for the most part his general picture of the world.

Foundational to these three stages which the child goes through are some generally held concepts of death which in themselves are mutually contradictory. First, death is not conceived of as a possibility for the self; but at the same time, the child fears that if strong adults die, what will he, the weaker child, do? Then death is never conceived of as resulting from chance or natural happening; yet the child many times feels guilty subsequent to a death, as though he were the secret slayer. This feeling of guilt is there even though death is personified as someone outside himself. These are a few of the ideas which, though paradoxical, are juxtaposed in the subconscious without contradiction.

Once we leave the pre-teens and enter the teen-age years, we begin to walk into a great unknown, scientifically speaking. If investigation is sparse regarding the pre-teens it is almost nonexistent in regard to the teen-ager's concept of death. One report I have found helpful is Robert Kastenbaum's *Time and Death in Adolescence*.

If we accept that by ten or eleven the child does have a concrete idea of death, we have to ask, "What happens to this idea?" Not only what happens to the ten-year-old's idea, but why is it that we as a society refuse to meet death as it is? Ours is a society which wants to forget death. Perhaps the answer lies in the teen years. At this point we must admit, with Kastenbaum, that the data we have are scarce. But with the evidence that we do have the following might be put forth as a tentative answer.

Most teen-agers do not want to think about death or anything associated with death. In general, they do not want to reflect much on their past or their future. Why? Probably because in the transitional stage they are going through, both past and future are sources of pain and anxiety to them. The fact of the matter is that they want to put as much time as possible between themselves and everything associated with their own death. Thus it would be suggested that when they do enter their "future" they will do it with a bang and not a gradual whimper.

There are, however, some adolescents who do not fit this picture, who are consciously concerned with both death and their remote future. This minority, amounting to about 15 percent, seem to be doing quite a different thing psychologically than are their peers. Instead of keeping the thought of their death separate from their present functioning, they attempt to structure their life in terms of goals and experiences far removed in time. The prospect of death is very much alive for them; it enters actively into the decisions they are making while still in the transitional world of adolescence.

When such a person ages, it is highly doubtful that he will face death in the manner of his peer who has characteristically refrained from including in his dominant life view the fact of his mortality. Having for years perceived himself within a long-range perspective that emphasizes the place of death in human values, he need not be disorganized by the realization that he has relatively little time remaining between himself and personal death.

How can we understand the adolescents who form the majority (and perhaps in the process understand our own feelings, if we have not been able to look at death)?

There are two well-known principles in psychology: First, the more ambiguous and unstructured a situation is the more the individual will impose upon it a personal structure made from his own needs and expectations. Second, emotionally powerful concerns do not evaporate when a person pays no conscious attention to them; rather they continue to operate unconsciously and influence behavior in various ways, many of which are unknown to the individual. Even when we say "Oh, I won't think about it," there is nothing to prevent the body from feeling and reacting to it. Thus are ulcers born.

If we apply these two principles to the situation of the adolescent's concept of death, we might say that the adolescent, in his transitional search-for-identity state, is uncomfortable with his memories of a past in which he lived in a role that he is now trying to transcend. He remembers himself as confused, inept, undifferentiated, bound to the wishes of others. As he attempts to repress these unacceptable aspects of his past, the feelings do not disappear but are available for displacement elsewhere, for other areas of expression. It would be difficult to imagine a more likely place for these feelings of cloudy dread and inadequacy to gather than in the subjective time field of the remote future. With all the realistic uncertainty surrounding it, the remote future stands as an unstructured "temporal ink blot," as it were, ready to receive the feelings the adolescent is trying to dislodge from consciousness.

It is as though the adolescent were seeking to throw away his past, but this unwelcome subjective entity acts as a boomerang, which meets him in his conception of the remote future. The "boomerang effect" leads him in his later years to attribute to the encroachment of death all the unhappy and terrifying feelings that have made his notion of the past unacceptable to him.

An adolescent lives in an atmosphere where old age is seen as useless and death is just another part of the survival of the fittest. In such an atmosphere and with such future prospects as old age, which he hates, and death, which he fears, he becomes what he wishes (projects) himself to be. The result is a circle: Those in old age are useless. Those dying are cast-offs of a utilitarian system. The adolescent sees this ambiguity and foresees it in pain and awkwardness, which he inherits from his past. When he reaches "old age" (whatever he has determined it to be), he finds it to be filled with awkwardness, fear, pain, frustration. Meanwhile another adolescent looks at him—and the process begins once again.

Adolescence is a personal revolution against the self. As with any revolution, much of the old remains, once things settle down. The self, though moulded and modified by the advent of puberty and independence, still is the same. Many of the basic fears, guilts, prejudices, and bases of pleasure are still intact. Intact too is the adolescent's view of death, as mentioned above. Somehow the circle begun at adolescence must be broken. Many times one's personal and theoretical understanding of death remains intact until it has to be faced as a result of a close death or a personal accident. One can benefit by thought, by thoughtful preparation. The circle can be broken by both thought and preparation.

Suggestions for Personal Reflection:

1. Are you comfortable with the knowledge that you will die?
2. Are you comfortable with death in animals? Could you talk freely about this with a child?
3. Speak to a young child, or teen-ager, about death.

Suggestions for Group Reflection:

1. How should children learn about death? What would you do or say?
2. Is your religion a comfort to you in thinking about death?
3. In your attitude toward death, which group of teen-agers were you in during your teen-age years?

CHAPTER VII—PREPARING YOURSELF

There's an apple tree outside my window.
The snow has fallen; the leaves blown away.
Children no longer shake its branches to catch
  forbidden fruit.
The deer no longer enjoy dessert and quiet shade
Yellow apples, spotted with brown;
Gray-black branches frozen against the moon.
I wonder which apple's next.

N. Kollar

The purpose of this book has been to help you reflect upon death. But reflection without action is useless. At this point I would like to offer some specific suggestions about preparing for death.

The first is that you must prepare for it in a very concrete way. If you have reached your middle fifties without making decisions regarding the details of your properties, body, etc., you are inviting chaos. The average wife is widowed at age 59. But at any age, lack of preparation is an invitation to disaster. Disaster can be avoided and those we love protected if we have some forethought. The forethought must include our specific wishes regarding monies, properties and funeral arrangements. If we neglect such preparation, everything will be left to chance—and to the greedy.

What happens when one of the spouses refuses to talk about death or its preparations? Much of what has been said in these pages depends on communication. If one cannot communicate with his/her spouse about death or life, many difficulties will arise, among the least of which will be funeral preparations. The solution to the communication problem here is the same as it is in the other areas of your life. It will be solved or remain unsolved in much the same ways. If worse comes to worse, you can make such minimal plans as filing instructions with a lawyer, funeral director, relative, or close friend. To keep peace, though, make sure your name is kept off any mailing lists and make the arrangements in person.

The arrangements to be made will reflect the complexity or simplicity of your life. "You die as you live," is also true of the actual funeral arrangements.

Funeral arrangements depend upon one's view of life, death, and funerals. Let there be no mistake about it, the funeral will reflect you and your values. The funeral in North America is unique in this world. The whole machinery of modern commercialism is manipulated to make the most of the emotional situations for profit. "Grief therapy," it is sometimes called. The pseudo-psychiatric terms are used to indicate that the "experts" in arranging these funerals can make death a happy event if they can control the atmosphere. These "experts" can also eliminate a great deal of the pain and guilt from death. The instinctive wishes of the relatives are analyzed and sublimated in order to sell them the corresponding remedy as expensively as possible. The whole process is based on the emotional vulnerability of the mourners who remain behind and wish to go back to ordinary life as soon as possible. The vulnerability of the surviving relative is more easily played upon as he is in a state of emotional disturbance. The process appeals to his vanity by manipulating the status symbol, and his desire to see the deceased live on in history as a famous person. The sense of well-being, stimulated by comfort, a sense of continuity, and security in life, is deliberately transferred to the dead person and the coffin in which he is put to rest. The "living standard" is consciously used to push up the "dying standard."

A new myth and vocabulary has developed surrounding the death and burial of an individual. It is this myth which may form the foundation of your practical choices regarding funeral arrangements. Underlying the myth are three assumptions. The first is that this style of burial is in the American tradition. But this tradition has been artificially created over the last twenty years. The second is the conviction that the burial industry gives the Americans what they want; in fact, only those "wants" are cultivated or excessively stimulated which are psychologically most vulnerable: man's vanity, his guilt complex, and the emotional disturbance when he is already upset. The third is the agglomeration of half-digested theories of certain popular psychiatry: Grief needs therapy. So they talk of "the dramaturgic role, in which the undertaker becomes a stage manager to create an appropriate atmosphere and to move the funeral party through a drama in which social relationships are stressed and an emotional catharsis or release is provided through ceremony."

The thrust of these pages is to offer a foundation for other choices than those of the great American myth. But to act contrary to the myth can only be done with advanced planning. Without this planning, the survivors are left open to the pressures of relatives, some funeral directors, and society in general. But if all is carefully planned in advance and responsibly implemented, the family and society will usually accept it. If people know you want a simple funeral, they will accept this wish when it is implemented by your survivors.

To help with advance planning, nonprofit funeral and memorial societies have been formed in some 120 cities in the United States and Canada. These societies cooperate with funeral directors, sometimes by having contracts with them and sometimes advising their members as to which firms provide the desired service. They also furnish contacts with medical schools and eye banks, for those who wish to leave their bodies for education or science, or their eyes for sight restoration.[2]

What kind of funeral do you want? Will it be elaborate? Simple? Will your body be present? These and a great many other concrete questions have to be asked. But they have to be asked within your view of what death and a funeral are.

One option is a simple burial. Here the body is removed promptly and with dignity for immediate cremation or burial. Afterwards, memorial gatherings of one sort or another are held. The emphasis here is upon the value of the deceased's life and memory.

Another option is a simple wake, church service, and burial. In this instance, all are able to see the body. The reality of death can be seen in viewing the dead body, which should not be overly "restored."

Finally, no one can place himself in your situation. You know your values, your view of death and life. It is within this framework that plans are made.

In the formulation of these plans, as with every other phase of life, there are people all too eager to plan your money for their personal prosperity. They offer all kinds of burial plans. There are few laws to control these practices. Because of this, these individuals can continue their victimization. No plan should be accepted in which you do not control all funds until time of actual need. The following safeguards provide a certain amount of security:

1. Beware of those offering cut-rate services.
2. Beware of phone or door-to-door solicitors calling themselves counselors.

3. Local firms of good standing do have a reputation to keep and thus can usually be depended upon.

4. If there is any doubt, check with your pastor; he is usually aware of the reputation of the local firms. The Better Business Bureau would be another check.

5. File your instructions with a funeral director who is content to have you or your bank control the funds for the funeral until services are actually rendered.

Your bank can be of great help in arranging your financial affairs. First is the decision as to the kind and the cost of the funeral you want to have; then the problem of payment arises. If you have adequate life insurance to cover the entire cost, then you merely designate the policy or policies required to pay for this service. The same principle applies if you have social security, veterans' or other benefits to take care of the expense of the funeral. However, if you wish to keep these benefits for your family and set aside funds for these expenses but still control them, talk to your banker. Usually he will be only too willing to set up a simple trust savings account with the funds specifically designated to be turned over to the appropriate funeral director upon your death.

The cost of a funeral should include all services. It is here especially that planning is essential. Because there are so many funeral directors in proportion to the population, they must sell as many extra services as possible to help meet expenses. When planning the funeral beforehand, one should get a written agreement as to *all* the services to be rendered and their cost. Usually the price of the funeral is set by the price of the casket. If the casket for a $500 funeral cost the director only $100 it does not mean he is making an exorbitant profit. The price quoted usually includes a long list of services. Thus you must ask about the services and decide which you do want and which you do not want. The funeral director will usually be reluctant to omit any of these services since they help pay his overhead. In addition some directors may refer to the simple service as a "pauper's funeral" or "county funeral." Such terminology is easier to deal with when there is no pressure than when a person is exhausted and nervous at a loved one's death. But whether it is a matter of language or of paying for all the services, pre-planning can avoid many of the pitfalls.

The checklist provided in Appendix "B" indicates the specific items to note in your planning. An important consideration in today's mobile society is the possession of cemetery property. Generally, unless you feel relatively settled, it is best not to buy any property until it is needed. People move around so much today that one must ask the reason for the burial plot. Children and relatives frequently move out of the home town so that there are few people who will regularly visit. Unless you are very stable, the chances are that you will move out of town because of your job, family, retirement, or other consideration. Many times people think that even though they move out of their home town they would still like to be buried there. At first glance this may seem like a fine idea, but the experience of others indicates that it might not be such a good plan. The cost of shipping is relatively stable, depending on distance and mode of transportation. The usual methods are railroad, air transport, and casketcoach. The cost of handling at the point of destination may vary from area to area. Ascertain beforehand the amount that will be added to the initial funeral cost and shipping charges at the point of destination. A lot of people regret their shipping of the body because of cost, the great emotional strain on those accompanying the casket, and the fact that few people actually visit the grave regularly once burial has taken place. Again, you know your own situation. What is offered here are some considerations you may not have thought of and which may help you make a more realistic choice.

Preparation for anything is always difficult. But anyone who has cooked a meal, painted a house, or traveled knows that without preparation the meal, the house, or the travel would never be achieved. If a child is to grow to maturity in *all* things, he must be prepared. If a mature person is going to exercise his intelligence over all things, even death, he must prepare.

Suggestions for Personal Reflection:

1. Read Appendix "B" and do those things which still remain.

Suggestions for Group Reflection:

1. Share your thoughts on Appendix "B."
2. What are some other ways you have found to implement preparation for death?

CHAPTER VIII
—OTHER THINGS: FAITH AND HOPE

All: When the storm has growled
Leader: They await him who will come
All: Him who will come
Leader: Him who will say: you come
All: Him who will say: come
Leader: And God will be with his sons
All: With his sons
  And this is the end.

(from a Gabon Chant)

Two people can hear the words of the Gabon chant and understand it in totally different ways. The death-situation is also open to such wide interpretation. Two people can be involved in this situation, yet experience it in totally diverse ways. One reason for such diverse interpretation has to do with the presence of Christian faith. Many times the words "Christ," "Paschal mystery," and "faith" are used in these pages. They are used with the conviction and belief that Jesus is of ultimate importance to all concerned and that He makes a difference in everyone's life. This view of Christian faith and Jesus Christ may be unfamiliar to some. One person, for instance, who read this book asked: "What denomination are you?" Such an inquiry calls for a consideration of the topic of faith.

Faith is a word we use frequently. We use it in many contexts and with many meanings. "If you believe you can do it, you'll do it." Or, "If you believe, you can move mountains." Belief here is seen as an instrument for action. Complete belief is somehow linked up with an energizing force that one can use at will: to make a chair float in the air or to convince another person to follow the will of the believer.

"Do you believe me? Really believe me?" or "He who

believes in me shall never see death." Belief in this instance seems closer to our word for trust or confidence. Somehow if I have faith in an individual I trust him. I allow him to see, hear, and think for me. Not completely, of course, but in those instances in which I put "faith" in him and trust what he tells me is true.

"Keep the faith, baby!" "What faith do you belong to?" are examples of faith as a list of formulas describing the community's "faith." It is the "credo," the belief listed in concrete detail and precise wording.

These are all various levels of meaning for the word *faith*. Basic to all of them is that faith is an attitude, a way of looking at reality. Faith is my attitude toward the entire cosmos. It is like a pair of glasses which enables me to see in a specific way. Some would say that everyone possesses faith of some sort. Everyone has his position from which he sees things, and this position might be called his faith.

But what we are speaking about is Christian faith which, somehow, through the conscious acceptance of Jesus Christ as Lord and Savior, gives one a different vision and experience of reality. One just "knows" things in a different way so that in the death-situation, for instance, one is aware of other dimensions to the sensible realities surrounding one. One knows that one's life is intertwined with that of Jesus. When it is said that the patient is representative of our sins or that we share with Christ the task of overcoming evil, these are real to the man of faith. Just as some people believed that Jesus Christ was Messiah when they saw Him in Nazareth, so too today we believe that what is real is more than what meets the eye. And faith's vision is present throughout sickness, death, and mourning.

This is not to say that the mind has no part to play in faith. Quite the contrary, we believe that truth is one and that what is experienced and what is believed are part of the reality. Faith channels the energy of mourning into a new wave of life. Our faith trusts in the One who has overcome all death and that this present death will also be overcome. And we believe in the resurrection of the dead, not alone but with the community of Christians.

This belief does not erase doubt. It does not take away the haunting blackness of the "what if" or the groping of the mind blinded by the senses. No, belief is not knowledge. We balance on the tightrope of belief by a constant "yes" and "no." If we ever let the complete weight of the "yes" take over, it is no longer belief but knowledge, a state of existence we will have when we are face to face with Jesus before the Father. On the other hand, a complete "no" also pulls us off faith's tightrope. It drops us into the pit of darkness where there is complete certainty. And the certainty is that of a life without light. There is no doubt here either because one is not exposed to the light. All is the reality of the senses or logic. We must realize that just as light needs darkness to be light so faith needs doubt. One cannot exist without the other.

Thus before death's door there is still fear. Fear for the individual near death, that there may be nothing. Fear for all concerned that their guilt may be a burden till death. Yet all believe that they celebrate a rebirth. They believe that once again it can be said, "Death, where is thy victory? Where is thy sting?"

Death's sting is weakened for the mourners because they have hope: hope that the dead lives in a new way and that his dying is not in vain. Hope is the constant attitude of the critically ill patient. In the sickness and death situation, hope should predominate. But what is the attitude of hope? What can be said about it? In particular how do we build up a hopeful attitude (habit) in life so that at moments of crisis we do not despair?

"Now hope that is seen is not hope. For who hopes for what he sees?" (Rom 8:24). Man has been described as "thinker," "symbol maker," or "tool maker." There are so many descriptions of man. One way to describe him is as "hoper," one who hopes. He tiptoes along the narrow ridge between the disappearing "now" and the ever newly appearing "not-yet." And his basic stance, when he is true to himself, is that of creative expectation, a hope that engenders action in the present so as to shape the future.

Man the "hoper." Can man exist without hope? Without stretching his imagination to the "not-yet"? Without grasping with the fingertips of mind and will that which is not yet seen perfectly? And when he stretches, when he grasps, what is he grasping for?

I do not think man can exist without hope. At the same time I think it is necessary to understand carefully what I mean by the attitude of hope. Much of our daily life is influenced by our advertisements, political promises, and preachers of Utopia. Hope always strives for the "not-yet," but at the same time it strives for a human "not-yet." The world of cleaner-than-clean soaps, sex-appeal toothpastes, and perfect husbands leaves little room for humans. "Human" means limited. It means that although we brush our teeth with the sexiest toothpaste we may still only kiss the toothbrush, and that, when the perfect husband walks out of the *Cosmopolitan* magazine, he will have headaches, rough beard, and incomprehensible ideas. Limited. Imperfect. Human. Hope.

Hope is human hope. It imagines the not-yet as possible. But it imagines within the context of reality.

Reality demands that we are never complete. We are always desiring more, desiring to go beyond ourselves, to transcend the now to the not-yet. But reality also demands that our transcendence will not be into a land of eternal sunsets where all is sweetness and kindness. Within each of us are the emotions of all of us: love and hate, fear and security, anger and kindness, pride and humility. These and many more emotions are like caged animals which hunger for freedom. As soon as we give one its freedom to roam, another claws at the door to be allowed out. What all this means simply is that hope, whose nature is to imagine the not-yet as possible, must always do so within the context of our reality. Although we may desire to love perfectly there will always be emotions of hatred that pop into consciousness; that although we might be perfectly secure, fear will squeak into our security. Our hopes are not unfulfilled because they are not realized absolutely. When they are not realized absolutely, what is wrong is our expectations. We are desiring to be like gods rather than humans. The absolute is not attained by humans. We are always limited. We are always feeling these other impulses which might seem to indicate that what we hoped for did not come true.

Take, for instance, a person's hope for a good marriage, a healthy family, and sound interpersonal relationships with everyone he knows—he can hope these things come about in an absolute sense, i.e., that there is never any trouble and that he never feels hatred, displeasure, anger toward others, etc. His hopes are bound to be unfulfilled. The promises of his married love and family life will seem like dead birds heaped in a pile—worthless and stinking—because none of the hope-filled promises were fulfilled. Life can take on a terribly pessimistic stance because his expectations were not fulfilled. They never could be. They were not human. On the other hand, a person with the same hopes and desires can see his hope-filled promises fulfilled in the midst of human turmoil and mixed feelings. Is not our hope contextual? Does it not exist within the context of humanity in general and *our* particular humanity?

Hope imagines. Without imagination hope is dead. Hope plus a fertile imagination creates the freedom to see new horizons, to create new worlds. But confusion reigns if there is only hope without a fertile imagination. If one hopes without the tools of bringing these hopes to realization (one essential is imagination), he actually is slowly being entrapped by hopelessness. He can hope too hard. He can hope himself into an attitude of boredom ("What's the use") or of hopelessness ("It doesn't matter"). This can happen because his is not a real hope. He has never seen fulfillment. It can happen because he refuses to imagine. It can also happen because he sees his hopes as entirely dependent upon himself.

Hope depends on others. We in the West, and particularly in North America, are filled with the spirit of individualism. Everything depends on *us*. We must be able to get ourselves out of every situation. Like James, 007, Bond we have a death-defying escape for every death-filled situation. Just as he never escapes with the aid of others so we are never to expect others' help for our escapes. But is this true? Do we not need others for hope's fulfillment? Many times we make hope itself an absolute. What we hope for, we expect to be able to attain alone. The reality is that we need others as well as ourselves to fulfill our hopes. It is because of this reality that hope depends on others.

As can be seen, hope is an attitude which is relative. It cannot be absolutized. It must be contextualized within all the characteristics I have mentioned so far. Coloring the entire attitude is the ability to wait. To be able to wait is central to hope. If hope is for the "not-yet," those good things of the future which are difficult to achieve, then it must know how to wait. The hoping which can wait is the mark of growing maturity. However, I must distinguish two kinds of waiting: one, which waits because there is nothing else to do; the other, which is positive and creative. This latter waits because it knows what it wishes and what it must do.

The waiting we are talking about is positive and creative; it makes real wishing possible. When properly understood and exercised, it means the ability to remain fixed upon a goal, to cope with obstacles, to make detours when an immediate path is blocked, to be willing to take all the intermediate means that are essential to the attaining of the goal. It also means the ability to handle other wishes so that they do not impede the realization of the central wish.

To be able to wait, therefore, includes also the ability to handle hopelessness. It will not panic, like a child, at any and every appearance of the hopeless.

Positive waiting is not altogether passive. It is, rather, active, in the sense that it does not yield. It confronts hopelessness, acknowledges it, grants it its rights and proper domain, but does not yield to its assault. One of the qualities of waiting is that it accepts the need and reality of all intermediate worlds. One of these worlds is the world of the means that are necessary if we are to get to the world of ends. To be able to accept this conditionality is to be able to wait.

If I want to get somewhere I must take all the intermediate steps. We have all had the kind of dream in which, for instance, we skip intermediate stations on a railroad to arrive quickly and angelically at our journey's end. The unconscious, which is the place of the dreamer in us, cannot wait. It can indeed wish, but it cannot wait or act intermediately.

If that part of us which cannot wait acts in this way with regard to space and the leaping of intermediate spaces, its action with regard to time is somewhat the same.

The hoping part of man waits for a given moment and a given time. There is an extraordinary sense of real time and real timing in real hope, and the ability to wait through all the intervening moments. The uneducated part of man, the negative unconscious, does not know how to wait for the appointed moment and pretends that time is for lesser mortals than itself. This part of us, really the child's part, is imperious and eternal, using the language of eternity to conceal the fact that it cannot wait or hope.

Like a child we demand that our wish be gratified *now*. A child has no history; it is not aware of time. If the object of its desire is not present now—right now, the alternative is not hope but despair.

Our hope must be that of the adult and not of the child. Our waiting and wishing must also be adult. One who hopes well grows well. And our growth is a never-ending process.

It is with this hopeful attitude that we approach the crisis moments of our life. Our hope at death's door is based on the promises of Jesus that he who eats His body and drinks His blood shall have life eternal. It is based on the reality of *His* resurrection which is the fulfillment of the Father's promise. Our involvement in the death-situation does not take away fear, for it is always there; it does not destroy doubt, for it *must be* if faith will live; it does not erase pain, for we are human. But our involvement does bring forth hope which looks to what is not seen, waits for what is not-yet, but is confident we will see and it will be.

Suggestions for Personal Reflection:

1. List the ten most important things in your life. What are the three most important?
2. Why do you continue to live?
3. What do you hope for yourself? Your loved ones?
4. If you could construct the most ideal day in your whole life what would it be like?

Suggestions for Group Reflection:

1. Go to a funeral.
2. What did you see there?
3. What do you believe happened there and was happening?
4. What do you hope about death?

APPENDIX A

Following are a few of the many scriptural thoughts on death. The words which accompany the references are the first words of the selection.

Old Testament Readings:

Job 1:21, Naked I came from my mother's womb . . .
Job 19:1, 23-27a, I know that my redeemer lives . . .
Wisdom 3:1-9, We accepted them as a holocaust . . .
Wisdom 4:7-15, A blameless life is a ripe old age . . .
Isaiah 25:6a, 7-9, The Lord God will destroy death forever . . .
Lamentations 3:17-26, It is good to wait in silence for the Lord God to save . . .
Daniel 12:1-3, Of those who lie sleeping in the dust of the earth . . .
2 Maccabees 12:43-46, It is good and holy to think of the dead rising again . . .
Ps 49, Hear this all nations, pay attention all who live on earth . . .
Ps 73, God is indeed good to Israel, the Lord is good to pure hearts . . .
Ps 130, From the depths, I call to you Yahweh . . .
Ps 139, Yahweh, you examine me and know me . . .

New Testament Readings:

Acts 10:34-43, God has appointed Jesus to judge everyone, alive and dead . . .
Romans 5:5-11, Having been justified by his blood, we will be saved . . .
Romans 5:17-21, However great the number of sins committed, grace was . . .
Romans 6:3-9, Let us walk in newness of life . . .
Romans 8:14-23, We wait for our bodies to be set free . . .

Romans 8:31b-35, 37-39, Nothing can really come between us and the love of Christ . . .

Romans 14:7, If we live, we live for the Lord; if we die, we die for the Lord . . .

1 Corinthians 15:20-24a, 24-28, All men will be brought to life in Christ . . .

1 Corinthians 15:51-57, Death is swallowed up in victory . . .

2 Corinthians 5:1, 6-10, We have an everlasting home in heaven . . .

Philippians 3:20-21, Jesus will transfigure these wretched bodies of ours . . .

1 Thessalonians 4:13-18, We shall stay with the Lord forever . . .

2 Timothy 2:8-13, If we have died with him then we shall live with him . . .

1 John 3:1-2, We shall see him as he really is . . .

1 John 3:14-16, We have passed out of death and into life because we love . . .

Revelation 14:13, Happy are those who die in the Lord . . .

Revelation 20:11-21:1, The dead have been judged according to their works . . .

Revelation 21:1-5a, 6b-7, There will be no more dead . . .

Gospel Readings:

Matthew 5:1-12a, Rejoice and be glad, for your reward will be great in heaven . . .

Matthew 11:25-30, You have hidden these things from the learned and have revealed . . .

Matthew 25:1-13, Look, the bridegroom is coming; go out and meet him . . .

Matthew 25:31-46, Come, you whom my Father has blessed . . .

Mark 15:33-39, 16:1-6, Jesus gave a loud cry and breathed his last . . .
Luke 7:11-17, Young man, I say to you, get up . . .
Luke 12:35-40, Be like men waiting for the arrival of their master . . .
Luke 23:33, 39-43, Today you will be with me in paradise . . .
Luke 23:44-49, 24:1-6a, Father, into your hands I commit my spirit . . .
Luke 24:13-35, Was it not necessary that the Christ should suffer . . .
John 6:37-40, Whoever believes in Jesus has eternal life . . .
John 6:51-59, Anyone who eats this bread will live forever and I will raise him . . .

APPENDIX B

Part I: Death Without Preparation

The following is a helpful list for those faced with a death for which everyone is unprepared.

1. Seek help and advice from a lawyer, minister, or family friend before allowing a mortician to have the body. Most hospitals will keep the body for a day while such advice is being sought. (To give the body to a mortician increases his bargaining power and pressures the family into more costly arrangements than are necessary.)
2. With arrangements:
    a) Notify your mortician.
    b) Notify your minister; make details known as to type of service, time, date, etc.
    c) Go to morgue to identify body, if required.
    d) Notify relatives and friends.
    e) Newspaper notice should be prepared before the newspaper is called; this facilitates the procedure. The notice should include name, age, nickname if any; closest surviving relatives; special groups to which the deceased belonged; favorite charity, if gifts of this type are preferred to flowers; time, date, and place of wake and funeral service.
    f) Notify insurance company.
    g) Arrange with family or friends to answer the door and phone and to keep a record of calls.
    h) Arrange appropriate child care where necessary.
    i) Coordinate the supplying of food for the next few days.

j) Arrange for household needs.
k) Arrange hospitality for visiting relatives.
l) Select pall bearers and notify them (avoid men with heart or back difficulties or make them honorary pall bearers).
m) Notify lawyer and executor.
n) Arrange for disposition of flowers after funeral (hospital or rest home).
o) Prepare a list of distant persons to be notified by letter or printed notice and decide which to send each person. (Prepare notice for printing if desired.)
p) Make list of persons to receive acknowledgments for flowers, calls, etc. Send acknowledgments (printed, hand-written or both).
q) Check all life, casualty, accident, death benefits (Social Security, Credit Union, Trade Union, etc.).
r) Check promptly when all debts, installment payments, and date payments are due; call prior to due date if an extension is needed (some have insurance clauses that cancel them in case of death).

Part II: Remote Preparation for Death
(Continental Association of Funeral and Memorial Societies, Inc., furnishes convenient forms—two sheets—to provide survivors with a guide for attending to the legal, tax, funeral, obituary, and other matters after a death. They may be obtained by writing to 59 East Van Buren St., Chicago, Illinois 60605. They cost 40 cents per set.)

The following is a list of pertinent information to be kept in a handy location to assist those who must carry on in the event of your demise.

1. Make arrangements with some person to take care of the details and tell him/her where pertinent information may be located.
2. Name of Memorial Society to which you belong, address and phone number.
3. Mortuary of your choice, address and phone.
4. Data needed for the death certificate: full legal name, address, length of time at that address, sex, citizenship information, place of birth, marital status, social security number, parents' full names including mother's maiden name, armed service record.
5. Funeral arrangements preference: cremation, burial, bequeathal. If cremation is permitted, decide the method of disposing of cinerary: urn in niche, urn burial, urn entombment, scattering (if permitted).

    Body to receive: earth burial in cemetery or entombment in mausoleum. Indicate name and location of the place in each case listed above. If niche, lot, or mausoleum is owned or otherwise provided, include the details.
6. Indicate your preference for a service: memorial, body not present, or conventional (casket open or closed); for friends and relatives or a private ceremony (list stipulations and place); at church (give name), funeral home, your home, or other (list details).

    Describe service and indicate clergyman, music, etc. Indicate minimum and maximum for expense of funeral.

    If remembrance to church or charity is preferred, list where gifts should be sent.

7. Information for newspaper: Include length of time in community, occupations, organizations of which you are a member, schools attended and degrees earned, honors and military service, list of survivors to date, and request for gifts to go to a charity of your choice (if preferred).
8. List people to be notified of your death (list location of your address book if the list would be the same).

Part III: Business Affairs

In order to facilitate the handling of your business affairs, it is suggested that you keep in a safe place the following business information. The location of this information should be given to the person selected to take care of the details in the event of your demise.

1. List the professionals who assist you:
   a) attorney
   b) accountant
   c) banker
   d) investment counselor
   e) life insurance agent
   f) casualty insurance agent
   g) auto insurance agent
   h) doctor
   i) dentist
   j) eye doctor, other physicians
2. Business or occupation and address of company.
3. Social Security number.
4. Death benefits to which your survivors are entitled:
   a) Social security.
   b) Working benefits (where applies).

    c) Life insurance policy, number, name of company, etc.
    d) Accident and health insurance policy, number, name of company, etc.
    e) Vets. of U.S. Armed Forces benefits where applicable.
    f) If receiving service pension or disability pension, give details.
5. Do you own any property upon which you receive or are entitled to rent or royalties? (If yes, give details.)
6. Social Security benefits: Describe and include pension funds or any annuity you already receive.
7. List any property you own outside the state or country.
8. Describe any trusts you may have created or over which you possess any power, beneficial interest, or trusteeship.
9. Life, health, accident, auto and casualty insurance contracts: Show name of company and address, also face amount, beneficiary, who pays the premiums, and location of policies. Also explain any policy loans you may have.
10. Real Estate: List all property, who may own it with you if other than spouse; name, address, interest of each joint owner.
    a) Describe property, location, deed location, date acquired, and how.
    b) If real estate contract still owing, show name, address, and balance to date.
11. Stocks, mutual fund shares owned: List number of shares and type, company, account number, certificate numbers, location of certificates, and name of broker or company.
12. Bonds and debentures (same data as stocks and

add face amount of bond, interest rate, and type).
13. Mortgages and/or promissory notes owned: original amount, date made, name, address of maker, collateral, interest rate, location of documents, assignments or co-signers, etc.
14. Contracts to all real estate owned: full price, down payment, dates of contract, name, address of purchaser, interest rate, location of contracts, balance as of what date.
15. Cash, checking accounts: name, branch name and address of banks, account numbers, other signers on account.
16. Cash amounts with credit unions, savings banks and savings and loan associations: name, address of each depository, passbook numbers, type deposit, rate of interest paid, name of other signers on account, location of passbooks.
17. List any other type property owned and give details.
18. Liabilities: Make a list of all items that you owe as of date; include real estate, loans, long-term payment plans, time of payments, names and addresses.
19. List any lawsuits you may be involved in and any claims against you; write up full details of your involvement.
20. Name of person who prepares income tax form and location of income tax information.

APPENDIX C

Celebration for the First Anniversary of Death or All Saints Day

One year after the death of someone, those people who were close to him/her should gather together to share their reflections and a meal in the memory of the deceased. This should occur only on the first anniversary. On the Feast of All Saints, the same ceremony should be held annually.

The community gathered together should be small, 7-11 adults with children. A child is anyone up to twelve years of age inclusive.

The ceremony, prior to the meal, should be of 30-40 minutes' duration. This is important because of the children's attention span. If there are no children present, this portion of the ceremony can be expanded. The parents should not hesitate to explain what is going to occur and why it is occurring to the children before they come to the ceremony, even though questions will be asked by them during the ceremony itself. The children who are to ask the questions should be appointed beforehand.

Crying might prove difficult for some of the people to handle. Crying is a natural phenomenon and it should not be suppressed. At the same time, the group should not be allowed to get caught up in a morbid approach to death. Usually if people can relax with their own crying and that of others, the natural processes of group inter-action will carry the ceremony to its end. But, of course, some people have a difficult time relaxing.

Each individual should bring some fresh fruit or vegetable to the service. As they come into the home they can place the fruit or vegetables in an appointed place. These symbols of life itself will be given to someone in need after everything is over. (Even the poorest families should bring something to give.)

The meal should be prepared by all who will be present or in a way that is suitable to the customs of the area.

The leader, someone previously selected to lead the celebration (e.g., oldest son/daughter), should make sure there is wine and a candle present. The leader should also select a reading from the Scriptures during with the subject of life and resurrection.

Gathering: *Fruit and vegetables are placed in their containers as the people are greeted, coats hung up, etc. When everyone is present, all stand and a small glass of wine is given to them. The leader picks up his glass and begins:*

LEADER: To life: now and forever!
ALL: To life: now and forever! (*All take a sip.*)
LEADER: To those here in spirit and memory!
ALL: To life: now and forever! *(Take another sip.)*
LEADER: To the Spirit of God who first hovered over the water of chaos!

To the waters that bring forth life everlasting!

To life itself!

We say "Amen," "Praise and thanks," to you our Father.

Father, source of life, we are happy to be here.

You gave Adam a garden of life and happiness. "Not enough," he said. "More," he shouted.

You gave Noah an ark to ride the waves of death and destruction, a rainbow standard to wave over the chaos you offered to him and his family. "No," they said. "We want more."

And so Abraham, Moses, David, Solomon. And so a people were born: life given, chaos overcome, spirit instilled. And the people demanded more.

So much more.

Jesus said that enough is this: Father, only you and your life.

That is why we are here. To remember those who could not rest; who wanted more: life without end.

Grant us everlasting life: the life of spring flowers and cuddling kittens; of prophets and kings; of accepting families and understanding friends; of pounding hearts and excited breaths; of sunny days and freshly cut grass—grant us more life.

Grant us your life, the Holy Spirit, which lasts forever.

ALL: We ask this through him, with him and in him in the unity of the Holy Spirit now and forever.
LEADER: To life everlasting!
ALL: To life everlasting!
(Finish wine and sit . . . get comfortable)
(Those children who ask the following and those adults who respond should be chosen beforehand. These questions and responses are only suggestions.)

1. Why do we bring fresh fruit and vegetables?
   As a tree and plant gives us life by giving itself, so we should give life to others by sharing ourselves.
2. Why do we drink wine today?
   Today is a special day. We are celebrating *(mention names)* whose life we shared. On special days we have special drinks; that is why we have wine.

LEADER: Life is like the wine we drink. Only by sharing it can we be happy; only if it is consumed and others smile. Life is like the fresh fruit and vegetables—their life ceases that others may live. They live on in us. We cannot live the same way forever. Things change. Persons change too. We all die. Death is a part of life. That is why we are here today, to remember the death of those we love.

Scripture reading by one appointed (this should be an adult). This is followed by statements by adults and children:
I remember *(name of person)* because . . . *(some event, characteristic, gift, etc. which is a cause of his memory.)*
When it seems it is all finished the leader rises and asks all to do the same. All grasp hands and stand in silence for a short period of time (eyes closed). The leader should then ask everyone to open his eyes and

gently begin the kiss of peace in whatever fashion is most natural to the situation.

A meal follows. At an appropriate moment at the end of the meal, the leader lifts a glass of wine and says: May we all be here next year (in November? whenever the next occasion) in spirit if not in this life. To life: now and everlasting! *Some wine is taken.*

The leader then asks that the lights be dimmed and takes a lighted candle: I *(name)* am a Christian. I believe in the resurrection and the life.

The leader passes the candle to the right. Each person speaks in turn until the leader once again has the lighted candle. The leader says: May the light we have shared be a symbol of our life. As this light goes out may our life go on.

NOTES

Chapter 1

1 These criteria were recognized in American law (May 26, 1972) when "brain death" was equated with legal death by a Richmond, Virginia, jury.
2 Albert L. Meiburg, "A Protestant Point of View," in *Theological Roots for a Hospital Ministry* (Government Printing Office, Washington, D.C., 1966), R. E. Hunt, Leo Jung, Albert Meiburg. P. 34.

Chapter 3

1 Much of what follows is from my article "A Healing Church," *Homiletic and Pastoral Review* (June, 1968), pp. 778-83.
2 Stole-fees: the money paid during the Middle Ages to the priest(s) who anointed the individual.

Chapter 4

1 Dr. Erich Lindemann, "Symptomatology and Management of Acute Grief," *American Journal of Psychiatry*, 1944, #101, pp. 141-148.
2 Dr. E. James Lieberman, "Americans No Longer Know How to Mourn," *Potomac, Washington Post*, Dec. 20, 1970, pp. 6-10, 17, 25.
3 Portions of what follows immediately are reprinted with permission from my article "Grief & Rite," *Liturgy* (May, 1973), p. 3.
4 An excellent discussion of these emotions and their place in religious practice can be found in E. N. Jackson, "Grief and Religion," *The Meaning of Death*, H. Feifel, ed. (New York: McGraw-Hill, 1965).
5 Roch Carrier, *La Guerre, Yes Sir!* tr. S. Fischman (Toronto: House of Anansi Press Ltd., 1970).

Chapter 5

1. Much of what follows immediately is reprinted with permission from my article "Grief & Rite," *Liturgy* (May, 1973), p. 4.

Chapter 6

1. Much of what follows is dependent upon Sylvia Anthony, *The Discovery of Death in Childhood and After* (New York: Basic, 1972), originally entitled *The Child's Discovery of Death* (New York: 1940), C. W. Wahl, "The Fear of Death," and M. H. Nagy, "The Child's View of Death."
2. Nagy, *op. cit.* p. 82.
3. The material that follows, to the words, ". . . and with his friends forever," is adapted from *The Canadian Catechism: Come to the Father*, Grade One, Teacher's Manual, eighth week. Pp. 117-121. (Toronto: Paulist Press/Griffin House, 1966).
4. Nagy, *op. cit.*

Chapter 7

1. Jessica Mitford, *The American Way of Death* (New York: Simon and Schuster, 1963), p. 18.
2. A list of these societies, plus many helpful suggestions, can be found in Ernest Morgan, *A Manual of Simple Burial* (Burnsville, N. Car.: The Celo Press, 1971).